The
GIFT
of
VALOR

The
GIFT
of
VALOR

A War Story

MICHAEL M. PHILLIPS

BROADWAY

PRINTED IN THE UNITED STATES OF AMERICA

BROADWAY BOOKS and its logo, a letter B bisected on the
diagonal, are trademarks of Random House, Inc.

Visit our website at www.broadwaybooks.com

First edition published 2005

Book design by Michael Collica
Frontispiece photograph by Mark Edward Dean
Maps by Hadel Studio
Photograph on page 244 by Sara Joy Walters

Library of Congress Cataloging-in-Publication Data
Phillips, Michael M.
The gift of valor : a war story / Michael M. Phillips.— 1st ed.
       p.   cm.
   1. Iraq War, 2003—Personal narratives, American.
2. Dunham, Jason, d. 2004.   3. Medal of Honor.   I. Title.

DS79.76.P485 2005
956.7044'34'092—dc22
2005042007

ISBN 0-7679-2037-6

1 3 5 7 9 10 8 6 4 2

Valor is a gift. Those having it never know for sure whether they have it till the test comes.

—Carl Sandburg

CONTENTS

The
GIFT
of
VALOR

PROLOGUE | *Hand Grenades*

Husaybah, Iraq

THE MARINES KNEW.

Somewhere in this desert city, in one or two or ten of those flat brown houses, someone was waking up, kneeling down for prayer, and planning to kill Americans today. Maybe he'd launch a rocket into the U.S. camp and spray hot metal fragments into the warehouses where the Marines lived packed tightly together. Perhaps he'd rig an artillery shell to explode along the street where an American patrol would pass in the evening. He might load explosives into the trunk of an old Toyota and press the gas pedal to the floor when the Marine sentries opened fire at the camp gate. Or would he just crouch behind a wall with a machine gun and wait?

From inside the fortified camp, each Marine looked out at the angry city of Husaybah and wondered when and where and how. And whether he'd measure up when the time came.

So it was that in the spring of 2004, Corporal Jason Dunham sat behind the razor wire and sandbags wondering what he'd do if today was the day someone in Husaybah woke up, grabbed a hand grenade, and set out to kill *him*.

Raised in the village of Scio, New York, the easygoing Corporal Dunham stood six-foot-one, with a bodybuilder's chest and an infectious, lopsided smile that disarmed wary young women and crusty old sergeants alike. His temples were shaved close, in the Marine style, and the top of his head was covered by a dirty-blond burr so short that it erased the cowlick above his forehead. Inked into his right arm was the tattoo he got during boot camp four years earlier: a skull wearing a military helmet emblazoned with the eagle-globe-and-anchor Marine emblem. On his left arm was a black skull with fangs, and on his chest a spade from a deck of cards overlaid with a skull gnawing on an eight ball, a souvenir of the years Dunham spent guarding a submarine base in Georgia before he was sent to Iraq.

The twenty-two-year-old Dunham was, in the eyes of his fellow Marines in Kilo Company's Fourth Platoon, the poster child for the Corps. Yet he had been in the combat zone just a few weeks and so far hadn't experienced that moment of fear and elation, resolve and doubt that came with taking another man's life. As the leader of an infantry squad, he had nine other Marines under his command, yet he had never had to decide which of his friends to send toward the sound of gunfire and which to keep safer in the rear. It was an interval of uncertainty when young men hoped their cocky war tattoos were more than just decoration.

Inside Camp Husaybah, the men of Fourth Platoon slept side by side on narrow cots, their only privacy a thin mesh of mosquito netting or a draped poncho, their only reminders of life before war what they packed in their seabags. Dunham brought a blue Yankees cap, a dartboard, and a folding chair from which he held court. That day in March the corporal sat inside the warehouse barracks with his platoon commander, Second Lieutenant Brian Robinson, and guided the conversation to a favorite topic: how to deal with an incoming hand grenade. The Marine Corps published manuals that covered almost every eventuality in warfare, but had no formal advice for grunts—the Marines' affectionate term for infantrymen—who found themselves on the receiving end of a live grenade. Each man had his own pet theory, and Corporal Dunham unveiled his for the lieutenant. If the Marine managed to cover the grenade with his helmet, Dunham said, the helmet's bullet-resistant Kevlar material would blunt the blast. "I'll bet a Kevlar would stop it," Dunham said.

Brian Robinson had taken command of Fourth Platoon just before it shipped out for its second tour of duty in Iraq in February 2004. At Camp Husaybah, the Marines were still getting to know their new lieutenant, and it was there that they gave him the nickname Bull because of his resemblance to the gawky courtroom bailiff in the long-canceled television sitcom *Night Court*. When the conversation turned to hand grenades, Robinson, assistant manager of the building materials department at a Wisconsin home improvement store before he joined the Marines, thought back to photos he had seen at the Marine Corps school for freshly minted lieutenants. They showed a 7.62 mm bullet—the kind Iraqi insurgents fired from their AK-47 rifles—passing easily through walls and Kevlar helmets. "There's no way a Kevlar could absorb that blast," Robinson told Dunham. The Marines' bulletproof body armor fared much better, however. The lieutenant had seen pictures of a ceramic chest plate, called a SAPI plate, that absorbed seven AK rounds before it finally cracked open.

"You'd be better off using a SAPI plate and protecting your nuts and your neck," Robinson told Corporal Dunham.

The lieutenant showed Dunham what he meant. He held his right forearm across his upper chest horizontally, and his left arm across his abdomen, the way a football halfback takes a handoff. If the Marine lay on top of the grenade like that, Robinson said, the blast might shatter both arms, but he'd probably survive thanks to the body armor covering his vital organs.

Lance Corporal Bill Hampton, one of the senior men under Corporal Dunham's command, overheard Dunham and the lieutenant going back and forth about the virtues of their grenade theories. Hampton thought that if a grenade rolled his way the sensible thing would be to kick it or throw it away and hit the deck. He remembered an older Marine once advising him to drop face down on top of his rifle, tuck in his arms, and aim the soles of his boots toward the explosion to absorb the shrapnel. Hampton didn't bother stopping to join Dunham's debate.

One of the Marines cracked a joke about a lieutenant losing his arms, which caught the attention of Staff Sergeant John Ferguson, the top enlisted man in the platoon and Lieutenant Robinson's steady right hand. Ferguson was a stocky, serious veteran of both the intervention in Somalia and the invasion of Kuwait. From boot camp on, Marines were taught that their worst possible failing would be to let down the men beside them, and Ferguson, a thirty-year-old from Colorado, had already experienced the nerve-wracking responsibility of leading men into places they might never leave. The idea that a helmet would contain an exploding grenade struck him as naive. "It'll still mess you up," he warned Dunham.

"What about the helmet *and* the SAPI plate?" the corporal countered.

"It would increase your chance of surviving, but I don't think it would work," Ferguson said.

Dunham persisted. "I think it would work."

For Marines at war it was a mundane conversation, the battlefield equivalent of the discussions that college students back home might have about last night's keg party or cubicle dwellers might have over where to go to lunch. Idle chatter about life and death, forgotten by the next time Corporal Dunham's squad ventured out on patrol or raided the house of a suspected insurgent fighter.

But memories of that day came rushing back to Staff Sergeant Ferguson a few weeks later as he stared at an Iraqi insurgent stretched out in an open lot, his body stiff, his head cracked open and his black tracksuit wet with blood. Nearby was the spot where Corporal Dunham had lain a few minutes earlier, a halo of red oozing out of his head into the hard Iraqi sand. Dunham's helmet was ripped into bits of flimsy fabric and scattered all over the unpaved lane.

1 | *Kilo Company*

Husaybah, Iraq

CORPORAL DUNHAM DIDN'T play head games.

Life for the new Marines, the young guys still in shock from boot camp, was already tough enough, and Dunham didn't see the point of making them even more miserable just for kicks. But Jason's was a minority view, and it was a time-honored practice in the Marine Corps for senior enlisted men to mess with the minds of the boots, as the new guys were called. Marine commanders had in recent years tried to eliminate dangerous hazing rituals and had prohibited, among others, practices referred to in Marine Corps rules as wetting down, flopping, psychological sit-ups, pink bellies, thrashing, ordnance kisses, and Beretta bites. Commanders had also restricted the tradition of forcing Marines to do push-ups or run if they erred in small ways—calling a corporal a lance corporal, for instance, or dropping a magazine full of bullets. A senior Marine could order such punishment only if he himself did the same exercise at the same time. Nonetheless, most men in Dunham's battalion—Third Battalion, Seventh Marine Regiment, or 3/7 for short—would automatically drop and do thirty-seven push-ups if they let their rifle fall to the ground, even if nobody told them to do so. That was a matter of simple integrity, in the Marines' view. Captain Trent Gibson, Kilo Company's commander, and Lieutenant Bull Robinson, Corporal Dunham's platoon commander, did push-ups if they slipped up on the names of any of their Marines.

The crackdown on hazing and punitive exercise pretty much left senior Marines with head games—called "fuck-fuck" games—if they felt like having a little fun with the boots. The commander of Dunham's battalion, Lieutenant Colonel Matt Lopez, hadn't exactly barred fuck-fuck games. But he had warned the men that they shouldn't do anything to the junior Marines that they wouldn't do in front of the colonel himself to the colonel's own son. Nonetheless, recalling the humiliation they had put up with when they were boots, some senior enlisted Marines saw no reason to spare the next generation the same indignities. The tradition was rooted in the sharply defined military hierarchy. A Marine infantry battalion was divided into rifle companies, the companies into platoons, the platoons into squads, and the squads into fire teams. Third Battalion had 900 men and Kilo Company had 190. A fire team had just three or four. The Kilo Company officers beneath Captain Gibson were first and second lieutenants. The senior enlisted man in the company was a first sergeant, with a gunnery sergeant, staff sergeants, sergeants, corporals, lance corporals, privates first class, and privates below him in unmistakably descending order. The Marines took their hard-earned ranks seriously. They addressed each other by rank, and often men who ate, slept, and fought together didn't even know each other's first names. There was an underlying truth in the classic Marine joke:

What do you do if someone tosses a hand grenade at you? Call for a private and throw him on it.

Corporal Dunham wouldn't allow fuck-fuck games in his squad. But sometimes the senior Marines got bored and toyed with the boots anyway when Dunham was out of earshot. "Put that down," a senior lance corporal barked at a junior lance corporal, Jonathon Polston, not long after Kilo Company arrived in Iraq. Polston obliged and put down the socks or helmet or CD player or whatever he was holding. As soon as he did, the senior Marine changed the order: "Pick it up. Put that down. Pick it up." Then the command shifted again: "Come here right now. Too slow—go back. Come here right now. Too slow—go back."

The game continued until Corporal Dunham saw what was going on. "Knock that shit off," he told the senior man. "If you're going to talk to him, talk to him. If not, just leave him alone."

Dunham's humane leadership won him the undying loyalty of the boots in his squad. Pfc. Kelly Miller was especially impressed when, in early March, Kilo Company's Fourth Platoon was sent to help Lima Company at its base in Husaybah. Camp Husaybah sat hard against no-man's-land, a fifty-yard-wide strip of sand, rubble, and garbage separating Syria from Iraq and claimed by both. The disputed zone was edged by tall fences and wire. Shopping bags of black, blue, and white plastic snagged on the barbs and flapped in the desert breeze like socks on a laundry line. The crossing point was a narrow road blocked on the Syrian side by a red-and-white metal gate. Anyone who bypassed the checkpoints and tried to sneak across no-man's-land risked being shot by Syrian border police on one side or Marine camp guards on the other. The war was supposed to be in Iraq, but sometimes it leaked across no-man's-land.

To the north of the Marines' outpost the border stretched through farmland toward the Euphrates River, getting wetter and greener as it approached the slow-moving waters. Iraqi boys grazed their goats on the marshy riverbanks, and during harvest season pomegranates and nectarines hung low over the American infantrymen riding on tanks or Humvees. To the south the border quickly disappeared into sandy wastelands and parched wadis, where the shrubs barely outnumbered the land mines.

Dunham's squad was assigned the task of fortifying the sprawling camp against mortars and car bombs by filling sandbags and setting up giant, cardboard-lined metal baskets called Hesco barriers. The engineers used construction machinery to fill the baskets with sand to form a thick blast wall, as much as twice a man's height, and the grunts topped them with coils of razor wire. As a squad leader, Corporal Dunham could have ducked much of the heavy labor. Instead, he worked alongside his men for a hot, hard week, and his men gratefully took notice.

Pfc. Kelly Miller, who turned twenty-one a month after arriving in Iraq, grew up in Eureka, California, an economically struggling area amid redwood-covered hills. Kelly's father, Charlie, was a retired mail carrier who had settled quietly into a routine of babysitting for his grandchildren. Kelly's mother, Linda, was a confident, energetic woman who managed a doctor's office. They lived with their three children in a working-class neighborhood in a blue, three-bedroom, one-bath house the Millers bought for $16,000 in 1971.

When Kelly, the six-foot-one, 210-pound baby of the family, turned seventeen, he took a job bagging groceries at Safeway to earn some spending money, and he gradually worked his way up to weekend night-crew manager after high school. For fun, he and his friends would trap crabs off the end of the Del Norte Street pier or race their cars by Clam Beach. Often he'd just hang out with his girlfriend, who worked in construction after finishing high school.

One morning in April 2003, while U.S. forces were taking Baghdad, Kelly ended his shift at the Safeway and walked into the Marine recruiter's office at a local strip mall. He had long been curious to find out how brave he was and how he'd perform in combat. So he signed up for the infantry, the grunts. The recruiter drove him home to get his birth certificate and high school diploma. Charlie was surprised. Linda was dismayed. Two months later Kelly was in boot camp in San Diego.

Kelly was assigned to Third Battalion and shipped to its base in Twentynine Palms, California. In the 1920s, the area, in the rocky, high desert, had been a haven for World War I veterans whose lungs had been burned by mustard gas in the trenches. Now it was a vast base designed to train Marines to fight in the brutal terrain of the Middle East and Southwest Asia. Kelly quickly realized that while he may have finished boot camp, he was still a boot. He and the other junior Marines had to sweep the dirt at the base to make it look neat, and on demand they had to serenade the senior enlisted men with "You Are My Sunshine." During urban warfare training, the grunts at Twentynine Palms had to work their way through a mock city, complete with silhouettes of bad guys and innocent bystanders. When one of the new guys accidentally shot a civilian silhouette, all the boots in the squad had to write essays explaining why it was bad to shoot noncombatants. Miller paid another Marine five dollars to write his essay for him.

In Iraq, Miller and the other boots were the first ones assigned to working parties around camp. They had to guard the ammunition. When the helicopters dropped off crates of water at the Marines' base in al Qa'im, the junior Marines had to pick up the hundreds of plastic bottles that scattered around the landing area after the crates inevitably broke open. Worst of all, as far as Kelly Miller was concerned, they had to take shifts burning the feces of the 350 men at Camp Husaybah. Navy engineers, the Seabees, had built the grunts plywood outhouses called burnout units. A typical burnout unit had three holes in a row. The Seabees installed seats if they could find them; otherwise the Marines just sat side by side on the slivery wood. Beneath each hole was half a fifty-five-gallon metal drum. When a barrel got too full, Miller and Polston put on leather gloves, dragged it out of the back of the outhouse, doused the slop in Humvee fuel, and lit it on fire with a book of matches or flaming piece of toilet paper. Kelly and Jonathon watched to make sure it burned thoroughly, stirring occasionally with a metal pole and trying to dodge the bitter cloud of fetid smoke. When it burned down, the Marines added more fuel and stirred some more, repeating until only ashes remained.

Dunham had spent his first years in the Corps guarding the sub base in Georgia and transferred to the infantry when the U.S. invasion force was already fighting its way to Baghdad. He stayed in California training other Marines and ultimately joined Third Battalion's Kilo Company in September 2003, after the unit returned from its first tour in Iraq. The battalion had been home just a couple of months when the grunts got a warning that they'd be returning to Iraq in early 2004. Jason's four-year enlistment was due to end in July, but he was told that he would go with the battalion for the beginning of its new Iraq deployment.

The other veterans teased Dunham for having missed the invasion. They'd call him a boot or sometimes Uno, because he had only one ribbon to wear on his dress uniform, the National Defense Service Medal given to everyone in the active duty military after the September 11 attacks, even if they never saw combat. In Twentynine Palms, when it came time to gather the empty cartridges from the shooting range, some wise-guy combat vet would ostentatiously announce in front of Dunham: "If this is your first time deploying to Iraq, you're picking up brass."

Dunham shrugged off the boot jokes. He had trained as a machine gunner in infantry school, and he knew that leading a squad of riflemen was a different craft. A textbook Marine attack involved jets, helicopters, and artillery hitting a target from a distance, followed by mortarmen, machine gunners, and riflemen in an increasingly personal fight that ended with a charge into the enemy trenches. "For you guys who were here last year, good on you," Dunham told his men. "But I'm going to do my best to do the right thing and get us back home. If you see me slipping, let me know." He kept dozens of spare batteries in his pack to make sure all his Marines had enough for their night-vision goggles, and he diligently jotted down tips in a green, clothbound notebook he carried with him:

> *Enemy will withdraw unless 1st attack a success.*
> *Don't sep. females from family.*
> *Stay away from kangaroo rats.*

Dunham learned his new job quickly and quickly earned the trust of the veterans around him. In December 2003, Kilo Company spent ten days in the barren expanses of Twenty-nine Palms training to deal with the elusive guerrillas and angry civilians they'd likely find in the Sunni Muslim areas of western Iraq. Marines from another battalion dressed up as Iraqi fighters and civilians, some wearing cardboard signs that read "Female" to test the grunts' sensitivity to sex roles in Arab culture. The role players then barraged Kilo Company with realistic scenarios, from anti-American demonstrations to militant ambushes to weddings in which celebrants innocently fired their weapons in the air. The exercise highlighted the hornets' nest that awaited the battalion; at one point a mock Iraqi gunman took a shot from behind a restive crowd of civilians and provoked two Marine units into shooting at each other. The days were warm, and the nights bone-chillingly cold. One day after dusk, Sergeant Mike Adams discovered that his cold-weather gear had been left on a truck, and the truck was long gone. The Marines were issued double sleeping bags that fit one into the other like Russian dolls. Together they were toasty. But separately they weren't quite enough for a night in which temperatures dropped below freezing. Dunham gave Adams one of his bags and his camouflaged poncho liner. They both woke up unable to feel their feet.

The physical hardships of the Marine Corps didn't present a great challenge to Dunham, who got a perfect score on his fitness test. But he thought the Marines hurt themselves by making young grunts intentionally miserable. He hated much about boot camp and the drill instructors whose job it was to strip recruits of their civilian identities and forge them into Marines. Not long into the thirteen-week training at Parris

Island, South Carolina, he wrote an old friend from Scio, his hometown. "Hey, how's it hangin'? Not so great here. This is the stupidest thing that I've ever done. It's almost like hell, or at least close. I'd like to kill my DI's but I can't." At the same time Dunham loved being a Marine, and in the same letter he reflected happily on the fact that he had a good shot at being picked as an honor graduate and winning early promotion to lance corporal. He ended up ranked second in his boot camp class.

Still, the more he saw of the Marine Corps, the more firmly Jason believed that leading through intimidation wasn't just cruel, it was self-defeating. Dunham wrote an essay on the Marines for a freshman composition class he took at a community college near Twentynine Palms.

> *Through my experiences in the Marine Corps, the one thing that stands out more than anything else is the fact that Marines abuse their power. . . . [F]or some reason they have the need to make and watch other Marines do pointless and senseless things . . . Watching them sweat and become fatigued is considered good fun for most marines.*

Dunham identified three types of Marines: the spit-and-polish Marine who lives for the Corps, the overweight "dirt bag" who is out for himself and has no respect for rank or the Corps, and the "more relaxed but good marine." A Marine of the last type leads by example and "understands that people make mistakes, and that there are some things that really seem not to make much sense therefore he doesn't pressure his marines to completely abide by them. Usually this type of marine would ignore something Marines call fraternization. Thus being that Marines could not hang out with marines of lesser grade. Well, how are your marines supposed to trust you if they know nothing about you aside of work."

Indeed, rank meant little to Jason when he chose his friends. It was at a sergeant's wedding that he met his girl-friend Sara Walters, a nurse from Michigan. And he sought the company of the men whose lives he had under his command. Lance Corporal Mark Dean, a twenty-two-year-old mortarman, had joined Third Battalion when it occupied the quiet city of Karbala after the fall of Baghdad. He came home after the tour ended, took a few weeks of leave, and then re-ported back to Twentynine Palms in October. When he opened the door to his barracks room, he found it occupied by several corporals and sergeants, who bellowed at him for entering without knocking. "Sorry," Dean said. "I didn't know they'd moved y'all in. This used to be my room."

Corporal Dunham immediately introduced himself and was the only one of the senior Marines who offered to help Dean move his belongings to his new room. It was the be-ginning of a fast friendship, and soon Dean's wife Becky Jo, a teaching assistant at a day-care center near the base, was hear-ing nothing but stories of Dunham this and Dunham that. Becky Jo and Mark had met in high school in Owasso, Okla-homa, and married a few weeks before Mark shipped out to Iraq the first time. She had family in the military and knew it would be tough marrying a Marine who might spend ex-tended periods overseas. But she thought it would be tougher not marrying him. Becky Jo was immediately charmed by Ja-son's smile and struck by his genuine interest in meeting the wife of one of his men. Soon Mark, Becky Jo, Jason, and Sara were double-dating.

In January 2004, the month before the battalion flew to Kuwait, Dunham and the Deans drove to Las Vegas for a gambling weekend. They talked about the war, and Mark told Dunham that when he made corporal, he wanted Dunham to pin on his new double chevrons. The three of them played a drinking card game called "Fuck the Dealer," after which they went downstairs to the casino and hit the roulette tables. Dean and Dunham bet together, each putting ten dollars on black seven times in a row. Every time the ball landed on red. Finally Dean couldn't take it anymore. "Do you want to go with red?" he asked.

"Yeah," Dunham answered. "Let's go with red." It hit black. They gave up, Dean having lost a big chunk of his $750 biweekly lance corporal's take-home pay.

Jason spent a few days in February camped out on the Deans' couch as the battalion's departure for the war loomed. On their drive to the base one day, Dean was edgy about the reports of rising Army casualties in the area of western Iraq the Marines were going to occupy. "Are you scared?" he asked Jason. "Are you worried at all about where we're going to be going?"

"To be honest, I am," Jason said.

Mark tried to look at the bright side, telling Jason there was no better way to die than for one's country. "I'm not going to let any of us die for our country," Corporal Dunham responded. He borrowed a line from General George Patton and told Mark, "Always remember—why should I die for my country when they can die for theirs?"

In boot camp, a Marine is taught that he isn't really fighting for a country or an idea; he is fighting for the Marine to the left of him and the Marine to the right of him. Jason's concern for the men beside him, and their eagerness to follow his lead, caught the attention of his seniors in Kilo Company. At the end of 2003, Captain Gibson reorganized the company into four rifle platoons to make it more nimble for occupation and guerrilla warfare, rather than invasion. The captain held a National Football League–style draft to allow the platoon commanders to pick their men.

Staff Sergeant Ferguson, standing in as Fourth Platoon's commander before Lieutenant Robinson's arrival, spent a weekend rating 160 Kilo Company grunts. His top picks were Corporal Travis Struecker to lead First Squad and Corporal Dunham to lead Second Squad. Dunham didn't have combat experience, but Ferguson liked the way he treated his Marines. Dunham was close enough to his men, for instance, to know if a lance corporal didn't have his mind on his work because of girlfriend trouble. Ferguson was impressed that Jason could get men to follow him without yelling, without intimidation. Nobody doubted Corporal Dunham was in charge, and Dunham felt no need to remind anyone. In Ferguson's view, Dunham inspired performance just by being himself.

Ferguson selected Lance Corporal Joshua Carbajal, a tough, compact twenty-year-old from Newhall, California, to be one of Dunham's two fire-team leaders. When Carbajal joined the Corps, the senior enlisted men treated him and the other boots like loathsome animals. They'd scream, berate, and play mind games, and that's the way Carbajal led as well. He didn't want to know which junior Marines were friends with each other or what their families were like. He wanted to have a clear head unsullied by emotion when he sent men into harm's way. Carbajal liked Dunham and considered him the physical model of what a Marine should be. But he thought Jason was "just too nice of a guy" when it came to leading men into combat. It was a philosophical divide that sometimes turned into heated arguments between the two, and Marines in the squad got the impression that the rivalry ran deep and verged on dislike. But Ferguson wanted Carbajal under Dunham because Carbajal was a veteran of the invasion. He hadn't seen much combat—just dodged a few mortar rounds—but he had moved through enemy territory and occupied an enemy city, challenges that Dunham could then only imagine.

Dunham's other fire-team leader, Lance Corporal Bill Hampton, a blue-eyed, sandy-haired six-footer from Woodinville, Washington, shared Carbajal's view of how a Marine leader should act. Bill's parents had split up when he was three years old, and he grew up with his older sister and his mom, who did some housecleaning around town and worked as an organic cook for an elderly local couple. Bill earned cash for himself working the register and fry machine at McDonald's, and unloading plants at a tropical nursery.

Bill became fascinated by soldiering at a very early age and had childhood visions of catching bad guys. The military plan didn't sit well with his mother, whom Bill called a hippie. She had lost good friends in Vietnam and had picked shrapnel out of the back of her first husband, a Marine sniper who served there. She thought she could best fend off a military career by indulging Bill's early enthusiasm, and she bought him camouflage pajamas, toy knives, toy canteens, and toy guns. He wound up collecting real pocket knives and getting into trouble for carving his initials into the family entertainment center before he turned seven. His mother tried to interest Bill in opera and symphony, but ended up taking him to football games instead because that's what her son really wanted to do. Despite her efforts, Bill's attraction to military life didn't fade, and after high school he joined the Marines because his uncle had been one and because his grandfather, a former Navy man, told Bill, "Everybody else is a bunch of pussies." When Bill went to boot camp he got letters from his father saying how proud he was that his son had volunteered to serve. His stepmother wrote that if her own boys turned out like Bill she'd die happy. While other Marine recruits cried after the lights went out because they were homesick and desperately wanted out of the Corps, Bill cried because he was so proud to be there.

———

The barracks at Twentynine Palms resembled a college dorm, and Corporal Dunham's room was always a center of Kilo Company social life. The Marines would watch movies, shoot the breeze, and drink beer—they were allowed one six-pack apiece in the barracks. Dunham was particularly keen on a video game called Medal of Honor, which he played relentlessly and unsuccessfully for hours. In the game scenario, the player was a World War II American soldier fighting his way across Europe, almost single-handedly, in order to turn the tide of the war.

For the most part, Jason's life in the Marine Corps was a good time for a young man at the top of his game. Even when he was dating Sara from afar, Jason found it easy and irresistible to meet other women on the side, and he told his friends that he wasn't in the mood to settle down. The grunts were a hard-partying crowd, and one of Corporal Dunham's preferred drinking buddies was Pfc. James W. Barnes III. A machine gunner from Bartlesville, Oklahoma, Barnes thrived in combat but at home spat out the bit of Marine discipline. His platoon sergeant described him as "one of those Marines you put in a glass case with a sign that says, 'Break in case of war.' " Barnes had been a corporal once, but was demoted to lance corporal for going to a sergeant's house with a beer in his hand to discuss their differences of opinion. He was busted down again, to private first class, for making off with a smoke grenade and a dummy hand grenade from the firing range at Twentynine Palms. Barnes routinely kept a big wad of Copenhagen snuff in his lower lip and a plastic bottle at hand for spitting. Jason threw up the first time he tried it. But Jason's name was written on the wall of Barnes's screened porch as the holder of the record for longest keg stand, fifty-two seconds. In a keg stand, the drinker, aided by other partyers, does a handstand on top of a beer keg while an assistant holds the tap open in the drinker's mouth until he can't take any more. Jason broke the previous record by twenty seconds. When they got to Iraq, however, Barnes and Dunham spent less time together. Dunham turned more serious and was frequently working with his squad. Barnes found it harder to socialize without beer to lubricate the conversation.

As the date for shipping out for the war approached, many Marines took advantage of the alcohol they knew they'd be denied in Kuwait and Iraq. Lance Corporal Polston, then eighteen years old, got thoroughly drunk in the barracks and—on a dare—undressed and jumped into the empty bed of one of his platoon mates. Pfc. Kelly Miller ran off with his clothes, and Polston pursued him through the halls. Polston ended up knocking on Dunham's door, buck naked. "Hey, Corporal, have you got my clothes?"

"No," Dunham answered. "What the fuck are you doing?"

"Miller stole my clothes, Corporal," Polston explained as soberly as he could. A more belligerent squad leader might have made Polston write an essay detailing the dangers of underage drinking. But with the war so close, Dunham chose to ignore the incident.

Lance Corporal Jonhatan Covarrubias joined Kilo Company between deployments to Iraq and found that nobody talked to him much. When the other Marines did address him, they saddled him with the nickname Gummi Bear because of his portly physique. Covarrubias found Dunham more approachable and forgiving when Covarrubias, then twenty years old, was caught drinking and driving around Twentynine Palms at night wearing sunglasses. One sergeant threatened to bust Gummi Bear down to private. But Dunham just asked him to tell the truth about what happened. Covarrubias denied having had any alcohol, and Dunham accepted his word. Later Covarrubias confessed to Dunham: "I was drunk as fuck."

Dunham told him to get a hotel room next time he wanted to drink. "We all do stupid shit as long as we don't get caught," Dunham told him.

The day before Kilo Company shipped out for Kuwait, Covarrubias proudly introduced Dunham to his mother and eighteen-year-old sister. Later, Gummi Bear's sister put out feelers about Dunham. "No way," Covarrubias said. "I'm not hooking you up with a Marine."

Lieutenant Bull Robinson had signed up for the Marines immediately after hijackers plowed planes into the World Trade Center, the Pentagon, and rural Pennsylvania on September 11, 2001. *The country's going to war,* he thought, and he didn't want to be left out. But the week before his physical exam he jumped into a bar fight to help a friend and broke his hand. The Marines made him wait until it had healed before they'd accept him. He tried to take a fatherly approach to the men of Fourth Platoon. Before a weekend liberty in Las Vegas, he warned them: "If you have sex, protect yourself. If you drink, don't drive, and if you get in a fight, win." But it was hard not to be drawn into Jason's social orbit. At a platoon party a few days before they flew to Kuwait, Robinson brought burgers, chips, and booze, along with another lieutenant who served as his designated driver. Dunham talked Bull into doing a keg stand, and the other Marines held the lieutenant's legs while he drank upside down. Dunham tried to take pictures, but Robinson's designated driver stood in the way.

As departure day approached, Pfc. Miller got increasingly nervous and called his mother Linda, his voice choked with emotion. "Mom," he said. "I don't think I can be away from you guys for that long."

"Can I do anything to help?" Linda asked.

"Can you and Shannon come down one last time?" Kelly asked shyly. His mother and his girlfriend, Shannon Hiscox, drove fourteen hours from Eureka to Twentynine Palms, and Sunday morning they all ate breakfast at Denny's. Corporal Dunham happened to be there with Lance Corporal Dean and his wife, Becky Jo. Miller introduced his mother and girlfriend to Dunham, who promised he'd take care of Kelly in Iraq. Shannon thought that if Kelly was going with a guy like Dunham, he'd probably be all right.

That night Linda and Shannon barbecued steaks for Kelly at the motel and stayed with him in his barracks until 2:30 the next morning. "Mom, thanks for coming," Kelly said.

"At least I have this memory in case I don't come back."
Shannon and Linda went back to the motel. When they
woke up, Kelly had already shipped out.

––––––––––

The battalion's first stop was a camp in the Kuwaiti desert,
where the Marines lived in white, eighty-man Bedouin tents
and made sure they had all their gear in shape for the move
north into Iraq. Dean ran out of cash soon after they arrived,
and Corporal Dunham bought him a 550-minute phone card
so he could call Becky Jo a few last times. Mark used every
minute.

Just before leaving Kuwait for Iraq, Captain Gibson had
his Marines send a typed form letter home. It read:

> *I am sending out this letter because my Commanding
> Officer wants to make sure that all Marines in the Kilo
> Family stay in touch with someone in the United States.
> Besides, as the saying goes, in order to get mail you have to
> send mail. As you may or may not know, we have deployed
> to parts unknown in the recently liberated country of Iraq. I
> am doing fine.*

The letter had three multiple-choice sentences and the
Marines were instructed to circle their choices:

> *The food here is: GOOD, OUTSTANDING, or
> EXCEPTIONAL!*
> *I am being treated better than: HOME, BOOT CAMP,
> or EXPECTED!*
> *The weather here is just like: HOME, HAWAII,
> HELL!*

Jason circled GOOD, BOOT CAMP, and HOME. In the "please send" section, he wrote in: "Razors, snacks, baby wipes, magazines, AA batteries, phone cards, soap, lip balms, lotion, packaged tuna fish, and a partridge in a pear tree. Beef jerky, circus peanuts, Whoppers, cheap candy."

Fourth Platoon hopscotched from Kuwait to al Asad air base west of Baghdad to al Qa'im, the Third Battalion's Iraqi base, and to Camp Husaybah, the outpost on the Syrian border. Jason soon put his candy supply to work, stopping to hand out sweets to the Iraqi children. Some kids happily approached the Marines asking in broken English for money, food, or soccer balls. Some found themselves yanked back into their homes by nervous parents. Some just glowered at the heavily armed Americans roaming their streets. Jason frequently halted patrols to play street soccer with the children, and his Marines set up a security perimeter to watch his back while he joked around and flirted with the grade-school girls.

Husaybah, a flat city of perhaps 100,000 people, was a near-perfect square, about a mile on each side. The Marines named the street that edged the western side of town West End, the street on the eastern fringe East End. The tracks and train station of the Iraqi Republic Railroad bordered the southern road, which the Marines called Train. Market Street ran east to west near the northern edge of the city. Inside the square was a symmetrical grid of dirt residential lanes, broken up by a few cemeteries, schools, and mosques. Camp Husaybah, home to Lima Company and Dunham's platoon from Kilo Company, sat near the intersection of West End and Market Street, in the northwest corner of the city.

For the most part the patrols through Husaybah and neighboring towns, in Humvees and on foot, were intended to show the locals that the Marines were friendly and wouldn't back down from growing insurgent attacks. Many grunts felt that they were really going into the streets as bait, to lure the insurgents into exposing themselves so the Americans could unleash their overwhelming firepower in return. But for the most part in March 2004, the insurgents stayed concealed among the civilian populace, a source of enormous frustration for Marines trained to close with and kill their enemies. The deadliest risk for the Marines came from roadside bombs the insurgents planted and set off from afar with garage-door openers, cell phones, and radio-control devices from toy cars. The bombs were hard to spot until it was too late. One might be stuffed into the carcass of a dead dog or hidden beneath a shopping bag by the side of the street. A pile of rocks might conceal a Chinese-made rocket, ready to fire down the lane. Patrolling through town, the Marines had to wonder whether those cans in the road were markers to warn the locals away from a trap set for the Americans or just goalposts for a game of street soccer. Some Iraqis would wave as the patrols went by. Some would cheer when a Marine was wounded. To the Marines' befuddlement, some would do both.

Corporal Dunham and his men came under frequent mortar attack at Camp Husaybah. But Dunham never got into a back-and-forth firefight or took a shot at the enemy there. He came close shortly after the Marines began to take control of the area from the Army's Third Armored Cavalry Regiment. The Army troopers considered Husaybah a snake pit and usually passed through it in armored Humvees and Bradley Fighting Vehicles. They thought the Marines' plan to patrol the town on foot foolhardy. One night Fourth Platoon went on a joint patrol with Army Bradleys, walking behind the armored vehicles while helicopters hovered overhead.

Dunham and his men were in a dark alley when they heard rifle fire and saw an Iraqi rocket-propelled grenade fly out of the former headquarters of Saddam's Baath Party and slam into one of the Bradleys roaming Market Street. Corporal Struecker's squad was at the platoon's front and poured fire into the Baath Party building. Corporal Dunham's squad was behind Struecker's, and Jason was eager to get into the fight. "Will you get us up there?" Gummi Bear Covarrubias asked Dunham.

"Hell, yeah," Dunham said. "We're going to get some action right now." He herded his squad forward until they were crowding up behind Struecker's men. Dunham and Struecker, a big, blond twenty-one-year-old from Algona, Iowa, had an endless series of friendly rivalries—in darts, Yahtzee, spades, video-game boxing, anything. They'd egg each other on when they got edgy, bucking each other up with jokes. When Dunham pushed his squad forward, Struecker turned and gave him a what-the-hell-are-you-doing look. Dunham grinned back and complained, "There's no room."

"Then go back where you were," Struecker snapped. Lieutenant Robinson ordered Dunham and his men back to the rear.

After a nerve-wracking patrol, or even a boring one, the Marines liked to play violent video games, such as Grand Theft Auto, and watch war movies like *Saving Private Ryan*, about the search for a single soldier after D-Day, and *Full Metal Jacket*, in which a sadistic Marine drill instructor is killed by one of his recruits and grunts grow disillusioned fighting street to street in Vietnam. Jason adopted a mud-caked stray puppy, and one of his men, Lance Corporal James Castaneda, built a cardboard house for it. Lieutenant Robinson finally told Jason he had to get rid of the dog, but

Dunham kept an eye out for it while walking the streets of Husaybah.

Jason wrote home in the last days of March and teased his brother Justin about having vomited after a night out with some friends. "You guys take care," he wrote. "Don't worry too much Mom, I'll be home as soon as the time's right. Love you all."

Jason chose not to tell Dan and Deb that soon after arriving in Iraq, he extended his enlistment by five months so he could stay with his squad through the entire combat tour.

———

At the end of March, Fourth Platoon left Camp Husaybah and relocated fourteen miles to the east to the battalion's isolated desert headquarters in the rail yards at al Qa'im. Dunham's squad was ordered to guard the corner of the base where the Central Intelligence Agency spooks and Army Green Berets lived. It was fun duty. There was the glamour of hanging out with the special operations types, who had better food than the grunts. And there were no platoon sergeants or officers watching over their shoulders. Corporal Dunham set the schedule for guard duty and night fire watch, which involved sitting in plastic chairs on the sandbagged rooftop with a machine gun and grenade launcher ready to repel attacks that never came. On the ground outside, the Marines placed a claymore mine, a curved, rectangular device that on command would send a horizontal hailstorm of steel balls outward into the faces and bellies of any attackers. To avoid horrendous mistakes, the manufacturers wrote "Face Toward Enemy" on the convex side of each mine.

One day Corporal Dunham quizzed his squad on the First Marine Division's rules for the Iraq war. The division commander, a major general, had tried to distill his guidance for his men down to a few rules they could carry on a wallet card. The idea was to help them protect themselves without losing sight of the fact that the Marines' underlying mission was to make Iraq more peaceful and pro-American. Injuring or killing civilians, even in self-defense, could aggravate an already tense political situation and generate support for the insurgency. Each Marine was supposed to memorize these rules, which included "First, do no harm" and "You need to look at everybody here as if they are trying to kill you, but you *cannot* treat them that way." Miller, Polston, and the other junior Marines had the rules down pat. But Lance Corporal Hampton got them wrong. So Dunham decided that from then on the senior enlisted men, including his fire-team leaders Carbajal and Hampton, would have to take shifts standing fire watch as a punishment while the others slept. When Hampton saw the fire-watch schedule posted on the wall, he thought it must have been a practical joke that Carbajal was playing on him. So he wrote "Blow me" on the paper. Corporal Dunham was furious, but accepted Hampton's explanation that the note had been directed at Carbajal. Nonetheless, Dunham made the unhappy fire-team leaders pull guard duty, much to the amusement of the boots. Carbajal, in particular, resented being forced to do menial work he thought better left to the junior men, and he angrily let Dunham know it.

On April 10, Dunham's squad moved out of the special operations camp and back into the warehouse where the rest of Kilo Company lived at the al Qa'im base. The squad was put back into the company's regular patrol rotation and assigned a mission for the morning of Wednesday, April 14. Dunham had been on plenty of patrols in Husaybah, but

Lieutenant Robinson had always prepared the formal order. A patrol order was the most academic element of a squad leader's job, involving a multipage write-up that analyzed the likely course of enemy action, the position of friendly forces, the nature of the mission, the plan for maneuver and route, the logistics, the radio frequencies, and the meanings of various smoke and illumination signals. Lieutenant Robinson thought Dunham seemed nervous about his first combat patrol order; after all, two other squad leaders in Kilo Company had already been demoted for failing to live up to their commanders' expectations.

The night of April 13, Corporal Dunham sat at the plywood table in the Kilo Company command post, an office in the corner of the warehouse barracks. As usual, he was barechested, displaying his muscles and Marine tattoos. On the wall in front of him was a mosaic of spy-satellite photos of Husaybah, the neighboring town of Karabilah, and, to the north, the Euphrates River, with each individual house clearly visible. Dunham worked long into the night. Around midnight Dunham's fire-team leaders, Hampton and Carbajal, came in to see if he needed any help. "I want to do this on my own," Dunham explained.

So Hampton and Carbajal went to the chow hall and brought him back a cup of coffee and a cardboard tray of egg loaf and sausage. "Hey, we brought you some breakfast," Hampton told Dunham.

"Thanks, you guys," Dunham said happily.

Captain Gibson smiled when he saw Carbajal and Hampton bring Dunham the midnight snack. Gibson was thirty-five years old and had spent nine years as an enlisted Marine before attending college and officer candidate school. He always tried to remember his own days as a lance corporal and not to ask his men to do tasks for which he could not explain the purpose. He considered the squad leaders to be the heart of a rifle company. If the squads worked well—on the offensive, providing security, responding to attacks—then the whole company would work well when the bullets started flying. He thought Corporal Dunham had a lot to learn, but also had the willingness to learn it, and he considered Dunham a natural leader of men.

Captain Gibson himself never felt free of the relentless burden and joy of leadership. A brooding man with a shaved head, his men called him Captain America for his enthusiasm for the job. Gibson got homesick when he was away from Kilo Company and the brotherhood of grunts in wartime. He considered it the mark of a fine leader that his subordinates started taking care of him not because he asked them to, but because they knew it would help him do his job. Gibson thought about taking a picture of Dunham at the plywood table, working on his patrol order and the tray full of eggs his men had brought him. *What would I ever do if I lost a Marine like that?* the captain asked himself. But it was just one moment of many in the war, and he didn't feel like going to get his camera.

11 | *The Mahogany Ridge*

Scio, New York

THE MAHOGANY RIDGE, a chipped, rust-colored wooden building, stood near the railroad tracks at the intersection of Main Street and River Road. On a tall sign in the parking lot a bearded, pipe-smoking mountain man beckoned to drivers-by with a jug of moonshine. A smaller sign at the door announced that snowmobilers were welcome. A third sign on carved wood advertised the "Mohogany Ridge" as the "Friendliest Bar in Scio." The spelling was wrong, but the slogan correct. The Mahogany Ridge was the only bar in Scio.

Outside the bar was the only stoplight in Scio. Across the street was the only minimart, and a few steps up Main Street was the only general store, a rambling brown structure called The Store. Under the shelter of The Store's porch roof was a vending machine that, for $1.25, spat out mealworms, salted minnows, or live nightcrawlers for fishermen looking to dip their hooks in the lazy Genesee River, just across the tracks. A short way up the road was Scio Central School, the village's grade school, junior high, and high school all in one. Next to the two-story stone Gothic Revival schoolhouse was the playing field, a mosaic of overlapping athletic lines. The baseball and softball diamonds lay back to back with a common outfield and no home-run fence to signal the start of one field and the end of the other. The soccer field stretched across the outfield, just above the hardball players' second base. The bleachers behind home plate squatted on the running track, which skirted first base and cut through right field, center field, and then left field before coming around third base and back to the bleachers. It was on that diamond in the spring of 2000, shortly before he reported to boot camp, that Jason Dunham played the most extraordinary high school baseball game his coach or anyone else on the Scio Central School team had ever seen.

Jason played catcher that day against the team from Belfast, a town not far up State Road 19. On his first two trips to the plate, Jason hit a triple and a double. On his third at-bat, Jason pounded a fly ball over the running track that, in the fenceless outfield, scored as an inside-the-park home run. His next time up the wary Belfast outfielders moved back to the inside edge of the track, but Jason hit a shot that soared over their heads and landed in front of a clump of trees near the house in deep left field, for another home run. On Jason's final at-bat the bases were loaded with Scio runners, and the Belfast outfielders retreated to the far edge of the running track when they saw Jason step into the batter's box. Jason arced the ball to dead center field. It landed ten yards behind the nearest Belfast player and bounced into the infield of the softball diamond, an inside-the-park grand slam in a 22–12 victory.

Jason finished his Scio Central School career, in which he played catcher, pitcher, center fielder, shortstop, and second baseman, with a .414 batting average, a school record.

In 1822, thousands of Turkish troops landed on the Aegean island of Scio to put down an uprising by the Greek peasants who lived there. Word of the ensuing slaughter reached America, where Daniel Webster, already a famed orator and lawmaker, fueled the outrage over Scio's rape. "In four days the fire and sword of the Turk rendered the beautiful Scio a clotted mass of blood and ashes," Webster intoned in the House of Representatives. "The details are too shocking to be recited." Scio's plight caught the imagination of a small group of pioneers in western New York, who in 1823 decided to call their new settlement Scio in memory of the far-away Christians who had perished at the hands of marauding Muslims.

By the 1850s, this new Scio, pronounced "sigh-oh" and located eighty miles southeast of Buffalo, was a bustling town of 3,184 inhabitants with sawmills on every stream that turned trunks of ash, pine, and hemlock into lumber to be shipped to market on the New York and Erie Railroad. But a fire soon ravaged Scio's forests, and the villagers obstinately spurned the idea of building tanneries. The next-door town of Wellsville got the tanneries instead, and the lucrative factories a century later. Scio ended up dependent mostly on other towns for employment and had fewer than two thousand residents by the time Jason was born November 10, 1981, to Natalie Walker, a high school sophomore from Wellsville. Natalie was sixteen when an older boy she had been dating for a few months got her pregnant. The boyfriend insisted Jason wasn't his and refused to chip in to cover the baby's expenses. Natalie didn't argue with him; rejection was a familiar feeling for her. She hadn't seen her own father since she was five years old. She dropped out of school and moved into a two-bedroom, $375-a-month apartment across from the A-Plus minimart in Wellsville, surviving on welfare.

When Jason was five months old, Natalie met Dan Dunham at what became the Mahogany Ridge, then called the Red Fox. Dan was twenty-one and proud of his reputation as Scio's bad boy. He drank too much beer, got into a few too many fistfights, and played practical jokes the police didn't find funny. But he was also industrious, working long days at a dairy farm in Scio. He fell for Jason from the start, and he married Natalie three months after they met. She got pregnant immediately, and Justin was born in March 1983.

Life went smoothly for the couple for about a year. But then the marriage disintegrated amid alcohol, silence, and screaming, and the mutual recriminations grew so barbed that they couldn't be withdrawn. The one thing they agreed on when they parted ways was that the boys would be better off with Dan than with Natalie. They timed the divorce so that it took effect after Dan had adopted Jason. The judge granted Dan custody of both Jason and Justin and assigned Natalie visitation rights. But she used them infrequently and disappeared from view for long stretches. Over the years that followed, Natalie gave birth to two more children by two more men and lost custody of them as well.

Dan made do the best he could with the boys on the $600 a month he earned as a farmhand. The farm's owner was as much friend as employer, and Dan and the boys lived rent-free in an old farmhouse on the property. Dan took Jason and Justin on his rounds, perching them on hay bales while he tended the herd. When they got a little older, the boys played aliens in the woods with squirt guns, fished and camped along the Genesee River, and smashed pebbles to make black and blue paint. The boys took up all of Dan's spare time, and

he shied away from another marriage until he met Debra
Kinkead.

Many Scio residents considered Deb the village's least
likely match for Dan Dunham. She had grown up in small-
town Pennsylvania, given to high collars and prim suits, and
moved north to take a job teaching home economics at Scio
Central School. She stenciled flowers on the walls of her
classroom, where she taught sewing, nutrition, family decision making, and kitchen survival skills in a room equipped
with four ranges, four stainless-steel sinks, and a bank of ve-
neer cabinets. Deb and Dan met in 1986 while chaperoning a
school soccer game. There was snow on the ground already,
and Deb wore her heavy parka zipped to her chin and a scarf
that revealed only her pale blue eyes. That was enough for
Dan. *I'm going to marry that girl,* he thought as he drove back
to the farm. They went on a few dates over the months that
followed. In early 1987 Deb invited Dan and the boys to dinner at her tiny apartment. Dan brought a rose. Deb baked ba-
nana bread, and Jason and Justin, five and four years old
respectively, devoured it. At dinner Dan laid his cards on the
table: he and the boys came as a package deal. That was fine
with Deb, who had been told by a doctor that she couldn't
bear her own children.

Dan proposed four times. Three of those times he had
been drinking, a habit he gave up about five years later. One
marriage proposal took place at a bar. Deb ignored it. The
second came in the living room, and Deb let that one slide,
too. Dan blurted out another proposal at a stock-car race but
was distracted by a crash just as he popped the question. Deb
didn't bother answering. She finally said yes when he asked
her sober by the kitchen sink. They married in 1988, and the
reports of Deb's infertility quickly proved exaggerated. Kyle

was born in 1989 and Katie three years later. Dan and Deb
came to rely on each other completely, and their romance
never faded. Dan's neatly trimmed beard turned salt-and-
pepper; Deb's loose curls went from light brunette to red.

Deb threw herself into the role of mom. Jason was an in-
different student, without much taste or knack for school-
work. He loved sports, however, and Deb and Dan had to put
a hook-and-eye latch high on the kitchen door at the farm-
house when Jason was seven years old or they'd wake up to
the sound of Jason playing basketball alone at dawn. When Jason was in elementary school Deb took him outside to the
hoop and taught him to spell by playing PIG and HORSE, the
basket-shooting games, using other words from his teacher's
spelling list. She made him read *TV Guide* before he was
allowed to watch the TV itself. Her devotion was rewarded
with his affection. When Jason was in kindergarten, the
teacher had the children make Mother's Day gifts. Jason told
Deb: "I don't have a mother, so you can be my mother."

Natalie resurfaced on occasion, but sent no birthday or
Christmas cards. There were moments of anguish for the
boys, such as the time when Jason was six years old and Natalie didn't show up for a promised outing. "Do you think
she's stuck at the red light?" Jason asked Deb and Dan. For
the last half of the 1990s, Natalie lived with a boyfriend two
doors down from the Dunhams, yet her contact with the
boys remained intermittent. Jason and Justin would drop by
to talk or do odd jobs or ogle her boyfriend's Corvette. Natalie referred to Deb as "your mother" when talking to the
boys. Once in a while Natalie would take them to a lakeside
cabin for the weekend. During one such trip Jason tapped
her on the shoulder and asked, "When are you going to tell
me about my real father?"

"When you get a little older," she answered. Natalie had kept Jason's biological father abreast of his son's progress and for years had shown the man photos of Jason to see if they kindled any interest. They never did. She knew that she had often let Jason down, and she felt that telling Jason the man's name would only set him up for further disappointment. Her friends knew who Jason's biological father was, but none let it slip to Jason.

Jason grew to accept that Natalie may have been his mother, but she wasn't ever going to be his mom. Justin wrestled with the rejection, angry at Natalie and for years mistrusting of Deb's affections. For most of his life Justin assumed that Deb had adopted him when she married Dan. When he found out at age twenty that that wasn't the case, he was upset. He told Jason, who was then twenty-one. They both told Deb they wanted to be adopted, but Natalie wouldn't have allowed it.

When Jason was fifteen, Dan's employer sold his dairy farm and tore down the old house. He had offered to sell Dan the whole operation, but Dan preferred to take a job at one of the factories in Wellsville, driving a truck and working on a crane crew. So instead, for a token twenty-five dollars the farmer sold Dan a 1.7-acre parcel across the Genesee River where the town gave way to rolling hills of goldenrod and purple wildflowers. The Dunhams bought what Deb referred to as a modular home and Dan called a double-wide trailer. Deb got a sewing room, a treadmill, a bigger kitchen, and a wall clock that played "Killing Me Softly" on the hour. Trying to keep the house neat, she did constant battle against four children, an incontinent one-eyed spaniel, and two German shepherds, one of whose obsessive tail-chasing wore circles in the carpet.

In his free time Dan built stock cars from scratch, racing them on three-eighths-mile dirt ovals at fairgrounds around New York and Pennsylvania. After a few years he was diagnosed with diabetes, however, and limited himself to patching up during the week the cars his friends wrecked on the weekends. Jason worshipped Dan and loved going to the races and watching his dad work on cars. "My dad isn't a person who expresses himself emotionally often," Jason wrote in an essay for a writing class. "But you can tell when he's thankful for help, or when he's glad that I would go and spend time with him in the shop or out at the farm working with him. He would always try to help us out with any problems that we would have. For instance if I was going to the movies with a girl he would give me some money to pay for the both of us, even if the money was tight. He would always brag to his friends about us kids, and about things we've done good."

Jason was equally hardworking, holding down several jobs to pay for his car, an elderly Ford Tempo that Dan had put $600 of work into just to get it safe enough to drive. During the summer after his junior year in high school Jason would wake up at 6 a.m. each day to trim Christmas trees at a local farm. Then at 5 p.m. he'd start delivering for the Pizza King in Wellsville. And in his spare time he'd mow, weed, and trim for a woman down the road. One day Jason fell asleep driving between jobs, veered off the road at thirty miles per hour, and wedged the Ford between a tree and a telephone pole. He emerged unscathed, but the car was a total loss. He still owed money for it, however, so he kept the jobs.

The same work ethic extended to sports. While Jason

lacked academic ability, he had both natural talent and dili-
gence in the gym and on the field. He trained doggedly and
studied those who played better than he did to learn why. In
soccer, baseball, and basketball he led not by cajoling or or-
ganizing his teammates, but by showing them how well the
games could be played. Plaques and trophies filled the walls
and glass cases of Scio Central School. In many places were
engraved the names of Jason Dunham and his friends: most-
valuable players, record holders, all-stars.

The thirty-seven members of the class of 2000 were as
close-knit off the field as they were on it, a small circle of
friends who went through youth together, with Jason at their
center. He and Jud Lambert, buddies since before they were
ten years old, were in and out of each other's houses con-
stantly. Jason was friends with Jenny Crittenden and Heather
Brisbee from the time he was in grade school; he dated both
of them at one time or another. The school was too small to
support divisive social cliques. Parties were usually open to all
and often involved Jason and his friends cajoling someone old
enough to do so to buy them beer. Then they'd head out to a
clearing in the woods and light a bonfire. The police were
largely a benevolent presence; as long as nobody drove
drunk, they would usually give youthful offenders a warning
and a lift home.

Scio was a town where the worst imaginable things didn't
happen. People left their houses unlocked when they went to
work. They left their cars unlocked, too, and the keys in the
ignition. Everybody knew everybody, and they knew their
parents, too. In Jason's case, it was even harder to get away
with misbehavior; his mother taught school and there were
no secrets in the teachers' lounge. Even though Dan bragged
about his own exploits as a hard-drinking young man, he and

Deb tried to keep a tighter leash on Jason and Justin. Typically, though, Deb would ground them for a week for some infraction, and Dan would unground them two days later. Jason's smile could undo most punishments. What trouble Jason got into tended toward harmless pranks or mild deceptions. His junior year he decided it would be a good idea to dye his hair Scio Tigers blue for a big game. Deb forbade it, but Jason figured a temporary dye would be permissible, so he doused his head in food coloring. The more he sweated, the more the color ran, until his face and neck were a ghoulish blue as he sprinted up and down the court. His skin remained stained for days.

Deb couldn't sleep well until she knew all the kids were home, so she and Dan told the boys that when they got in at night, they had to stop by their parents' room. When Jason stayed out past curfew, Justin or Kyle would go to Deb and Dan's doorway and, lowering their voices, pretend to be Jason checking in. More often than not, Jason was out with a girl. He was meticulous about his clothes, but went shirtless whenever he could get away with it. He knew the effect his smile had on girls, teachers, parents, and friends, and he brushed his teeth three or four times a day. In the third grade Jason handed a note to a little girl at school. "Come on and kiss me baby," it said, a line he'd heard Dan use on Deb.

Jason's charisma and looks proved a painful contrast for his younger brother Justin, a talented artist but less endowed with natural prowess when it came to romance and sports. Justin was born with a cleft lip and palate, and the girls seemed to go out of their way to tell Justin how attractive they found his brother, while the boys praised Jason's athletic skill. During Jason's senior year, he and Justin rode together on a bus back to Scio from an away basketball game. Justin had spent much of the game on the bench, while Jason starred as usual. The other players teased Justin about his failures and Jason's successes. When the boys were alone, Justin complained bitterly that he was tired of living in Jason's shadow. "Don't worry about what other people think," Jason told him. "Just do what you do. The only person you have to impress is yourself."

After high school Justin tried a year of graphic design classes, but ran short of money. He worked at a Kmart, ran the roller coaster at an amusement park in Ohio, and sold vacuum cleaners door-to-door. At the amusement park he met his fiancée Amy, and the two moved into her parents' home in the woods in Slippery Rock, Pennsylvania.

Jason's most serious girlfriend was Melissa Whitcher, a quick, pretty woman two years ahead of him in school. At first it was a bit awkward, since Melissa was a freshman in college and Jason just a junior in high school when they started dating. She didn't want to attend Jason's junior prom; instead they went to an amusement park. Melissa soon moved to Myrtle Beach, South Carolina, where she managed an ice cream store and later vacation beach rentals. The relationship blossomed, nonetheless, and when Jason was at his first posting as a Marine, guarding the sub base in King's Bay, Georgia, he'd borrow a car and drive more than five hours to Myrtle Beach on the weekends. On Melissa's twenty-second birthday, in March 2002, Jason suggested they skip out on a family gathering, pick up a twelve-pack of beer, and go for a walk on the beach. It was high tide, and there wasn't much beach to walk on. Jason dropped to one knee and asked Melissa to marry him. He had teased her with mock marriage proposals before, and Melissa wasn't buying it. "Come on, Jason, get up," she said. Then he took out the ring. She didn't hesitate; she always knew they'd end up together.

Melissa's mom and Deb planned the wedding. Jason wanted Dan to be his best man. But as the date approached Jason's feet got cold. He called it off once, then rescheduled, then called it off again. The last time they were together as a couple was when Jason was about to report to Twentynine Palms, a year after they became engaged. They spent two weeks in Myrtle Beach, then Jason got into a rental car, picked up a Marine buddy in Kentucky, and drove west with $150. They ran out of money along the way, and Melissa wired them cash. Over the months that followed, the phone calls became less frequent, the commitment less firm. Jason fell out of touch for several weeks, making up a story later that he had been deployed to Kuwait during that period. But the truth was he was in California dodging the painful breakup that had by then become inevitable. In October his relationship with Melissa was over.

That month Jason met Sara Walters, a blonde, twenty-three-year-old nursing student from Zeeland, Michigan, at a wedding in Las Vegas. It was a small affair: just the couple—both of them Marines—Jason, Sara, and two other friends. Sara and Jason first spotted each other at the ESPN Zone bar, where Jason, a fervent Yankees fan, was watching the final game of the American League championship series against the Red Sox. He turned, waved, and went back to the game. That night the wedding party drank at Coyote Ugly, where the waitresses danced on the bar and Sara was captivated by Jason's charm. They eventually made it back to the hotel, and

Jason made a pass at her. "I know how Marines operate," she scolded him. "I've heard stories about you. You're going to have to work a lot harder than that."

Jason did. Sara returned to Michigan, finished nursing school, and eventually landed a job tending to stroke victims, the comatose, and other critically ill patients. She loved caring for people and thrived on the fact that her patients depended completely on her for their most basic needs. Sara and Jason talked long-distance every day, but she was still leery of him until he showed up for a ten-day visit at Thanksgiving. Sara lived with her parents, and they set the ground rules: Jason slept on a futon in the basement. The night he arrived they went to a friend's bachelorette party at Tiki Bob's bar. Sara gazed at him and confessed, "I think I'm falling in love with you." Jason gave her a wide smile and a hug, but said nothing. "Are you going to say anything to me?" Sara asked indignantly.

"Oh, yeah, I love you, too," he responded with a grin.

The Marine recruiter spotted Jason in the Wellsville Kmart the summer before his senior year in high school. Scio had a history of sending its sons and daughters into the military; a photo board in one hallway at Scio Central School showed graduates serving in the armed forces. Dan had spent a few years in the Air Force before returning to the farm, and he felt military service had helped him make the rocky transition from adolescence to adulthood. Besides, he and Deb didn't have the money to send the boys to college, and good factory jobs were getting harder to come by in the Scio area. Not that Jason had either the appetite or the aptitude to go to college straight out of high school; he once confessed to Deb that if he had done so he would have spent the entire semester at parties and flunked his courses. But Jason did picture himself going back to school eventually, and the Dunhams believed the GI Bill would be a good way for their son to pay for school when the time came. The military also seemed a good outlet for Jason's boundless energy. The elite Navy SEALs appealed to him, in particular, as did the military police, since he thought about becoming a New York state trooper some day. So when the Marine recruiter told him the Corps bred the toughest of the tough, he didn't have to work very hard to get Jason to enlist, with his entry delayed until after he completed high school.

Since Jason was only seventeen at the time, he had to get Dan and Natalie, his legal parents, to give him permission. Two Marines came to the house to talk to Jason, Dan, and Deb together. One of the recruiters discouraged him from signing up for the military police because they were just "glorified security guards." The Marine convinced Jason he would get the physical and leadership training he was looking for if he became an infantryman, a grunt. Jason agreed, and Dan signed on the bottom line. Both he and Deb were proud of Jason's decision. War, in the days before the September 11 attacks, seemed only a distant possibility.

Later, Jason and the recruiter took the papers to Natalie, who was working at a hardware store in Wellsville. "You're sure you want to do this?" she asked Jason. The military isn't like college, she said; you can't just quit if you don't like it.

"Yep—this is what I'm going to do," Jason replied curtly. He returned home fuming that Natalie had questioned his resolve in front of the Marine recruiter.

Jason even persuaded his friend Jenny Crittenden, who had been thinking about going into the military anyway, to sign up with the Marines. "Oh, come on," he urged her. "You can't be a wuss and go to the Air Force. You're a tough girl." Jenny took the physical exam and was sworn in. But she backed out before boot camp because the intelligence job the recruiter had promised her didn't turn out to be available. During their high school graduation ceremony in the spring of 2000, Jason tried to get Heather Brisbee to enlist, too. He didn't manage to talk her into it. But later Jason did persuade both Jenny and Heather to get tattoos.

It was in November 2003 that Jason got the news that he and his new unit—Kilo Company of Third Battalion, Seventh Marines—would be shipping out for Iraq early the following year. Jason telephoned Scio Central School from Twentynine Palms, and the front office put the call through to Deb's classroom. Jason tried to sound casual, but Deb had heard on the radio that morning that more Marines were being deployed to Iraq. "I just thought I'd call you," Jason said.

Deb cut him off. "Are they sending you to Iraq?"

"How the hell did you know that?" Jason asked.

Deb flipped the handset upside down, lifting the mouthpiece above her head so she could still hear Jason talk, but Jason couldn't hear her cry. The students in her Bachelors' Cooking class stared. "Here's the good news," Jason said. "I get to go home for Christmas."

In December Jason flew from California to Michigan, picked up Sara, and drove her car through Canada to Niagara Falls. They spent the night with his old friend Jud Lambert, who was studying at a university there. Jason told his parents that they had been stuck for hours at the border crossing and couldn't make it all the way to Scio that evening. But in reality he and Jud spent the night drinking. Sara was too nervous about meeting Jason's parents to drink much and was uncomfortable that he had lied to them. Later, she held Jason's hand while he threw up outside Jud's apartment, then tucked him into bed on the sofa.

Deb thought Sara seemed nice and that she and Jason made a cute couple. But Deb remained very close to Melissa, his former fiancée. Deb and Melissa went out for coffee one day over the holidays, and Jason tried to tag along, insisting that he and Melissa were friends again. "Not yet," Deb said. She found Sara a little too eager to take Melissa's place at Jason's side and was put out when Sara suggested it was past time for Deb to "cut the apron strings" with Jason.

Everyone wanted time with Jason during the holidays, and Jason tried to please them all. Jud and the rest of the old gang wanted to meet at the Mahogany Ridge for drinks. Jason approached Melissa there, but she was still too hurt about their broken engagement and brushed him off. Justin and Amy, who had just announced their plans to marry, wanted time alone with Jason and Sara. Kyle Dunham, then a four-teen-year-old freshman with braces and a wispy black goatee, wanted to play video games with Jason. Kyle was an honor-roll student and earned his spending money babysitting for five dollars a day. But he dreamed of becoming a Marine machine gunner like his older brother.

Jason took his sister Katie to lunch at the Texas Hot restaurant in Wellsville to celebrate her eleventh birthday. Katie, who had long blond hair and wore wire-rim glasses, owned a T-shirt that read, "I'm the good one. My brother's the brat." The reference was to Kyle, though, not Jason, who spoiled her with gifts and treats. He'd do push-ups with Katie on his back and hug her affectionately in the school hallways.

Jason told her she wasn't allowed to have a boyfriend until she turned forty, and tacked on the additional condition that she had to be married before she could date. "Jason, don't worry about that," Katie would tell him. "I'm not going to." For Valentine's Day one year Katie made cookies and a card for each of the Marines who bunked near Jason in the barracks. Funny and fearless, Katie seemed the most likely of the Dunham children to succeed her father behind the wheel of a stock car. But she was also an avid reader of books about dogs, foster children, and preteen babysitters. Before she read anything, however, she'd check the last page to make sure the story didn't have a sad ending.

The Dunhams went through the usual Christmas routine. They shoveled a path to the barbecue and grilled steaks in the snow. On the mantel Deb hung up the cross-stitched stockings with the kids' names on them. But the war loomed over the holidays, and she hid her tears from Jason as she took the stockings down again after the twenty-fifth. *He's right there,* Deb berated herself. *Why am I crying? This is stupid.*

As they headed out the back door into the snowy driveway one day, Jason turned to Dan and said that if he didn't make it home from Iraq, Dan should use the military insurance money to build himself a garage and a back porch for Deb overlooking the hills, and to send Kyle and Katie to college. And, to Dan's surprise, Jason said that if his wounds left him incapacitated, he didn't want to remain on life support. "Dad, don't let me lay there for a day if I'm going to be that way forever."

Not long afterward the family sat in the living room watching *Blackhawk Down*, and Jason pointed out a machine gunner firing frantically from a Humvee turret at swarms of Somali fighters. "That's what I do," he said.

Deb was appalled. "You have to tell them you need a different job."

"Why?" Jason asked.

"There's not enough protection," Deb insisted.

Jason laughed. "Mom, I can't do that."

Deb walked out, unable to watch more scenes of gunfire and gore. As she went through the doorway to the kitchen she turned back to Jason and said coldly, "You want your dress blues."

"Yep," Jason said.

"And you want a full military service."

"Yep."

Nothing more was said. They both knew they were talking about Jason's funeral.

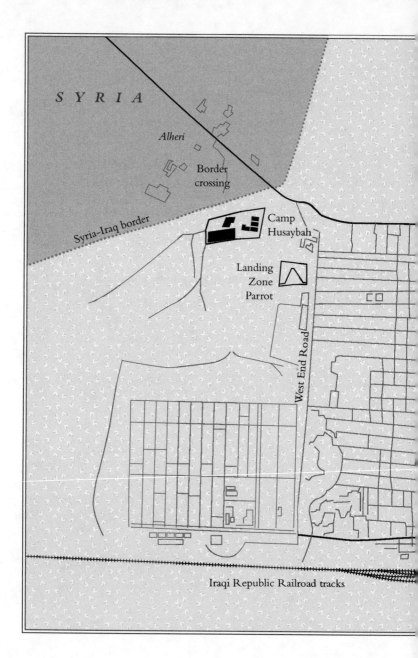

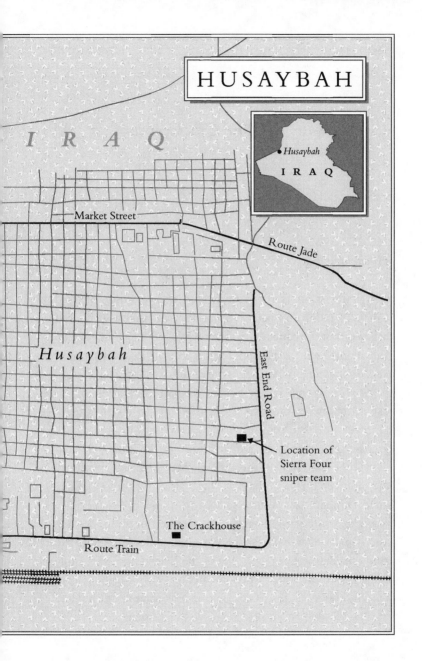

HUSAYBAH

Husaybah
IRAQ

I R A Q

Market Street

Route Jade

Husaybah

East End Road

Location of
Sierra Four
sniper team

The Crackhouse

Route Train

III | *The Crackhouse*

Husaybah, Iraq

ON THE MORNING of April 14, Captain Gibson ordered Corporal Dunham's patrol to conduct an ambush drill as it rolled out of the battalion base at al Qa'im. The patrol—called Kilo Four-Two for Kilo Company, Fourth Platoon, Second Squad—traveled in two high-back Humvees, big jeeplike vehicles with open beds and benches to carry infantrymen. For extra firepower, they were escorted by two gun trucks, Humvees that had rooftop turrets armed with machine guns, grenade launchers, and antitank missiles. Including the ten men in Second Squad, the captain, Staff Sergeant Ferguson, the Humvee crews, and a few others along for the ride, Corporal Dunham had twenty-seven lives in his hands. The day was sunny and warm, but the crushing heat of the Iraqi summer hadn't yet arrived. As the Humvees pulled over onto the sand outside the front gate, one of the Marines yelled, "Contact right," to indicate that enemy fighters were attacking from the right side of the road. The grunts scrambled out and dropped to their stomachs or kneeled with their unloaded rifles at the ready. Then, working in teams, they rushed a hundred yards into the desert toward the imaginary enemy while their squadmates provided imaginary cover fire, chanting, "Butter-butter-jam, butter-butter-jam," the sound of three-round bursts from an American M16 rifle. Their foes defeated, the grunts leapfrogged back to the Humvees the same way, one man running as another man covered him.

It was a routine Kilo Company Marines rehearsed every time they left camp. But Corporal Dunham's squad had been out of the patrol rotation for a few weeks, and the rust showed. While the Marines were counterattacking to the right side of the road, they forgot to cover the left side, and Captain Gibson caught the mistake. If this had been a real ambush, Gibson lectured Dunham and his men, they could have been wiped out from behind. The captain felt bad about berating Dunham; he knew the corporal led his squad well. But insurgent attacks had intensified recently as the Iraqi fighters tested the newly arrived Marines. One Kilo Company Marine had died in a rocket-propelled grenade attack four days earlier, the company's first man killed in action, and the captain felt the loss like a fresh wound. Corporal Dunham gathered his squad and gave a few quick orders to ensure that next time no approach would be left unguarded.

Then the men of Kilo Four-Two loaded live ammunition into their weapons, climbed into the Humvees, and headed into the worst day of fighting since the battalion's return to Iraq. Over the next three hours, street battles erupted across Husaybah and neighboring Karabilah, each linked to the next by design or chance.

The day began with a bang. Then another.

The first mortar landed at 9:38 a.m. near Camp Husaybah,

twenty-four miles by road from the base at al Qa'im. The shell hit just east of what the Marines called Landing Zone Parrot, a tarmac expanse where medevac helicopters set down to retrieve the wounded. Iraqis still considered LZ Parrot the parking lot where, during moments of quiet, they lined up to cross into Syria to earn some easy money. The Iraqis outfitted cars and trucks with huge gas tanks that jacked up the rear ends like hot rods. They'd fill up with cheap Iraqi gas, wait hours to clear customs, cross into Syria, sell the fuel on the high-priced Syrian market, wait a few more hours to clear customs, and return home.

The second mortar landed moments later next to the raised dirt road that ran north along the border from LZ Parrot toward the Euphrates River. Neither round came anywhere near the Marines, who were getting used to hit-and-run shelling of their base. A couple of days earlier insurgents had fired seventeen mortar rounds, apparently aimed at Camp Husaybah. The shells instead pounded the nearby Iraqi Civil Defense Corps headquarters and the border crossing itself.

But even when the mortars fell wide of the mark, the Marines tried to find out where they had come from. So at 9:50 a.m. First Lieutenant Dave Fleming led a handful of Marines out of Camp Husaybah on foot to read the craters. Like Captain Gibson, the twenty-nine-year-old Fleming had been an enlisted Marine before he got his degree and became an officer, and he still had a grunt's toughness beneath his genial sense of humor and Bugs Bunny tattoo. While the Marines were in Kuwait in early 2003, awaiting orders to attack into Iraq, he had his men psych themselves up for combat by beating each other bloody on the hard desert floor, scraping, kicking, and gouging in a few-holds-barred free-for-all. "Get him in the trachea or the carotid artery," he'd yell at his men. "Pull his nose back so you can get your arm around his throat."

An 82 mm mortar round is about the size of a two-liter Coke bottle, and looks like a small rocket, with an elongated, vaguely oval warhead perched on top of a short, finned stem. When the shooter is ready to fire, he drops the round into a metal tube, which is usually planted in the ground on a heavy plate for stability. The angle of the tube and the amount of powder attached to the mortar determine how high and how far the explosive flies. It takes experience to calculate the right charge and angle to hit the desired target, especially when the shooters—as was the case with the insurgents in Husaybah—feel the need to escape before the people they're shooting at come looking for them. Lieutenant Fleming's job was to plot the path of the mortars in reverse: he would find the impact craters left by the two mortars and try to figure out where the shooter had been.

A long mortar shot usually requires a flat trajectory, like a swimmer doing a racing dive, and leaves an uneven crater with black skid marks in the dirt in the direction from which the round was launched. The remains of the fins are almost always thrown straight ahead on impact, allowing the crater analyst to connect the dots and plot the line of flight. A very high shot might land straight down, creating an almost perfectly round crater, much as an Olympic high-diver makes almost no splash entering the water from the ten-meter platform. Craters from close shots are tougher to read, since they don't leave telltale direction indicators. But a shooter close to his target is also more likely to be spotted. The craters themselves are usually just a few inches deep if the round hits hard-packed dirt or tarmac. It's the jagged shrapnel that flies upward and away from the warhead that makes the weapon so dangerous.

Lieutenant Fleming found the first crater near the landing zone, read the scorch marks and fin placement, and sighted along the path that the projectile had flown. With his compass, he took a directional reading and then drew the flight path on his map of Husaybah. He did the same with the second crater. If one shooter fired both rounds from the same place, then the point where the two flight paths crossed should have indicated the spot where the mortar tube had been. Lieutenant Fleming looked at his map and wasn't surprised to see that the two lines crossed at the grounds of the Husaybah city hospital. The Marines had taken fire from the hospital compound before and figured the Iraqis felt they could shoot at the Americans from a hospital without much fear of retaliation. Lieutenant Fleming got a kick out of reading craters; it felt like detective work. But he also knew there wasn't much point in racing to the hospital to hunt for the perpetrators. By the time he calculated where the mortars had come from, the shooters would be long gone.

The insurgents had that major tactical advantage over the Marines: they were usually the ones who got to decide when and where to fight. The Iraqis would set up a mortar tube or plant a roadside bomb or lay a machine-gun ambush and trigger them at the times of their own choosing. The Marines tried to even the odds by being as unpredictable as possible. Company commanders sent sniper teams out at night to ambush Iraqis as they dug holes for bombs. Lieutenants varied patrol schedules. Even twenty-year-old lance corporals made spot decisions about whether their fire teams would turn left or right, walk up one street or down another.

While Lieutenant Fleming was out reading craters, Second Lieutenant Brad Watson, commander of Lima Company's thirty-eight-man Third Platoon, was inside Camp Husaybah wrestling with the same problem. Watson thought that if every patrol began and ended at the camp, they'd be easy targets for enemy ambushes. So he decided to seize a building inside the city that morning and dispatch his patrols from there. Watson, a sandy-blond twenty-five-year-old, had been a news producer for CNN when the four jetliners were hijacked on September 11, 2001. He quit television and joined the Marines. Lieutenant Colonel Lopez, the battalion commander, nicknamed Watson "Wall Street" because he showed up at the base in Twentynine Palms wearing camouflage fatigues and carrying a leather briefcase.

Watson's platoon had already been hit hard in Husaybah. Just a week earlier one of his foot patrols had run into three roadside bombs in a period of an hour. His Marines had been on Market Street, the commercial heart of the city, handing out toys and soccer balls to children and announcing a new curfew via loudspeaker. One Marine was killed and six others wounded. Watson himself suffered minor shrapnel wounds to his legs and torso and was evacuated to the trauma unit at the battalion's base in al Qa'im and then to al Asad, the next hospital up the medical ladder. He returned to duty at Lima Company's outpost in Husaybah three days later and found that his Marines, thinking him gone for good, had already packed his belongings and piled them up on his cot to be shipped home.

The April 14 mission was Watson's first since he had been injured, and he wanted to throw the insurgents off balance. His plan was to have his Marines move by foot out of Camp Husaybah, seize a derelict building that the troops called the

Crackhouse, search it for weapons, and then use it as a base
for patrols around southern Husaybah over the next six to
eight hours. For extra security, the lieutenant dispatched a
sniper team to find some perch not too far from the Crackhouse and watch over the patrols as they scoured the streets
and homes.

The Crackhouse was a three-story, dirt-colored building
on Train, the road that edged the rail line on the southern
side of the city. Perhaps a hotel or apartment block at one
time, its first floor consisted of abandoned storefronts covered
by metal shutters. The top two floors had balconies in front,
an internal central stairwell, and a few stray box springs in
otherwise empty rooms. The rooftop offered a good view of
the railway station, the surrounding neighborhoods, and
even some of the buildings on East End road.

Corporal Daniel Lightfoot, one of the platoon's squad leaders, wasn't happy about Watson's plan and thought it symp-
tomatic of the excessive eagerness sometimes shown by young
second lieutenants. The corporal considered the Crackhouse a
deathtrap. The Marines had taken fire from the building on
several occasions and had found a Chinese-made rocket inside
one of the shuttered ground-floor stores. On the way to the
Crackhouse, Corporal Lightfoot spotted seven or eight Iraqi
men of military age lounging outside a house and laughing
aloud. Lightfoot sensed they were laughing at the passing
Marines. He had his men press the Iraqis up against a wall for
a pat-down search. The Marines found no weapons, but at
least the Iraqis stopped laughing.

While the Marines went room by room through the
Crackhouse, Lieutenant Watson called "Squad leaders up"
over the radio and took Lightfoot and several others to the
flat roof to get an overview of the area. Watson noticed a

large pile of scrap lumber and kindling on the rooftop, perhaps three feet high. He thought nothing of it, since he had found it common for Iraqis to keep spare firewood on their roofs. Lieutenant Watson reviewed the planned patrols: he wanted two squads to hit the streets, while Lightfoot's men held down the fort at the Crackhouse. Lance Corporal Kevin Roshak, the platoon's lanky, sandy-haired radio operator, took Watson's digital camera, walked to each corner of the roof, and snapped photos of the streets below for the company's intelligence files. Then he took off his radio backpack and sat cross-legged a few feet from the roof's edge, ready to relay messages among the squads, Watson, and Lima Company's command post at Camp Husaybah. The lieutenant walked to the ledge and looked out at the town through a pair of binoculars. Then he leaned over to Roshak to radio Lima Company.

Before he could say a word, the woodpile blew up.

The concussion from the bomb—a 155 mm artillery shell hidden under the scrap wood—nearly knocked Lieutenant Watson off the roof, and he heard the same penetrating ring and felt the same disorientation he had experienced with every bombing in the past week. Corporal Lightfoot, standing with his left foot on the ledge that ran around the roof, felt a rush of heat all over his body as if he were being groomed by a massive blow-dryer. At first he felt no pain. He crouched down and checked his torso, arms, and legs to make sure there was no blood dripping out. Then he thought he heard some gunfire and turned away from the ledge to take cover. As he stepped down he felt a stabbing pain in his left foot that reminded him of the time he had broken an an kle snowboarding. He stumbled to one knee, stood up again, and hopped on his good foot into the small hut that sheltered the top of the staircase.

Corporal Lightfoot pogoed down to the third floor, where he crossed paths with Lance Corporal Chris Dosek, who was racing the other way to see what the explosion had been. Dosek asked Lightfoot if he was all right. "No, man—take my boot off," he responded. "I can't feel my toes." Dosek kneeled down and lifted Lightfoot's injured foot onto his own knee. He unlaced the boot and carefully slid it off. Lightfoot told him to take it slow with the sock, although he consoled himself with the thought that if his toes hurt this badly, they were probably still there. Dosek rolled the black sock off and exposed a one-and-one-half-inch by one-inch hole on the top of the corporal's foot. Lightfoot was alarmed to discover he had an unobstructed view of the bone and tendon running to his big toe.

"Aw, shit," Dosek said. He put Lightfoot's bloody boot in his own backpack for safekeeping.

The bomb blew Lance Corporal Roshak, the radioman, to his right and sent a stinging pain through his left shoulder. Then the left side of his face went numb. "I'm in trouble," he said to himself. The air smelled of burnt carbon, a biting stench even stronger than the odor of the rifle range. Roshak lay on his right side and moved his legs to make sure they worked. A variety of scenarios ran through his head: Had his ear been blown off? Was the radio handset somehow lodged in his neck? He knew something was very wrong but didn't dare touch his neck for fear of making matters worse. His hearing was dulled by the blast, yet he could still make out Lieutenant Watson calling his name from beside the hut at the top of the staircase. "I'm down," Roshak responded. "I'm hit." He sat on the rooftop, leaning on one elbow, until another Marine ran onto the roof and pulled him twenty feet into the hut.

When Hospitalman Third Class Tivey Mathews reached the top of the stairs, he saw a crowd of Marines gathered around Roshak and gawking at the nine-inch-long, jagged wooden stake that jutted out of Roshak's head, just below his left ear. The spike was wedge-shaped, perhaps three inches wide at its base, and studded with bent nails. The Marines were discussing whether to pull it out. Mathews was a corpsman, the Navy's equivalent of an Army medic, and, like all corpsmen, was known as Doc. Doc Mathews quickly put an end to the debate over Roshak's stake. He had no idea whether the wood had hit an artery or not. If it had, the stake itself might be plugging the hole and might be the only thing keeping Roshak from bleeding to death. Roshak asked Doc Mathews whether his ear was still there.

Hospitalman Third Class Joseph Lynott, called Doc Chops for the long sideburns he had once had, was assigned to the Marine engineers. But for excitement he liked to patrol Husaybah with the infantrymen, and the grunts were always happy to have a spare corpsman along just in case. At the Crackhouse, one corporal even invited Doc Chops to help search the building for weapons, and he was only too glad to tear open one of the metal shop shutters with bolt cutters and a crowbar. He was watching a Marine take a ride on the moped belonging to a passing Iraqi policeman when he felt the jolt of the explosion above and found his arm and shoulder covered with dust and debris. Doc Chops ran inside and heard voices above calling, "Corpsman up." He sprinted to the roof and arrived in time to help Doc Mathews walk Lance Corporal Roshak and his giant splinter down to the third floor.

The corpsmen cautiously wrapped the pointed end of the spike in white gauze, then spooled the bandage around Roshak's neck to stabilize the wood. "How the hell did that happen?" Doc Chops asked Roshak, silently cursing himself for neglecting to bring his camera on the patrol.

"I don't know, Doc," Roshak said.

A minute or two after the bomb exploded, the Marines in the Crackhouse began taking rifle and machine-gun fire from nearby houses. Lieutenant Watson poked his head out of the rooftop hut to see if he could spot any of the insurgents and then fired a single shot with his pistol to try to force the Iraqis to duck down while he ran out to retrieve Roshak's radio. The Marines saw gunmen in white robes firing from a white house on Train and muzzle flashes at a building perhaps 150 yards away, where a large tapestry or rug hung airing on the roof.

After helping Lightfoot, Lance Corporal Dosek picked up his weapon, a light machine gun with a plastic, 200-round ammunition box hanging underneath, and settled in by a third-floor window. There was gunfire zipping all around, but he wasn't sure where it was coming from. A boxy gray sedan drove by the building, west to east, and the Marines swung their muzzles toward the car. Dosek leaned out the window and screamed, "Stop, stop—don't go nowhere." Dosek was in an unforgiving mood toward Iraqis because of the casualties the platoon had suffered over the previous week. He figured the men in the car had probably detonated the bomb that had just injured Lightfoot and Roshak. The car stopped. "If he moves, shoot his ass," Dosek heard a Marine yell. Then someone, somewhere, fired a shot, and the Iraqi continued driving slowly eastward. The Marines poured a barrage of bullets and grenades into the sedan's passenger side. Dosek fired about a hundred rounds at the car in a matter of a few seconds.

When the shooting quieted, the Marines searched the sedan, but they found no weapons inside. Doc Mathews ran out of the Crackhouse and found the older Iraqi man in the passenger seat dead. The driver, a young man, was badly wounded. Doc Mathews opened the driver's door and lifted him out from behind the wheel, and a Marine propped the Iraqi up as they walked away from the bullet-riddled car. Doc Mathews followed behind, cutting open the man's shirt with a pair of scissors. The doc saw a large wound in the back of the man's shoulder and another bullet hole in the side of his ribs. He dressed one of the wounds on the move.

When the gunfire erupted above, Roshak and Lightfoot were downstairs waiting for a lift to the landing zone. The noise from the machine guns was deafening and echoed through the building. The medevac Humvees soon arrived, and the wounded Marines climbed into the rear bed. A staff sergeant handed Lightfoot his rifle, which he had forgotten upstairs, and said, "You're security for the back of the Humvee." Doc Mathews helped lift the injured Iraqi driver into the Humvee bed next to Roshak. The man spoke plaintively in Arabic, and Roshak heard the word "Allah" enough times to know he was praying. The Iraqi keeled over onto Roshak, bleeding on the Marine's pants and flak vest. Roshak didn't want the Iraqi to bump into whatever it was that was stuck in his head, and he tried to prop the man back up. But the Iraqi kept tipping over as they drove to the landing zone.

Lieutenant Watson estimated the firefight lasted forty-five minutes. He never saw any enemy fighter go down, but he figured that since the Marines shot off about seven hundred rounds, they probably hit someone.

———————

When the Humvee arrived at LZ Parrot, a familiar corpsman whose name Lightfoot could never remember approached and asked how he was feeling. "I'm in fucking pain," Lightfoot said.

"I've got something for you," the doc teased. "Do you love me, Lightfoot?"

"Yeah, I love you," Lightfoot answered. The corpsman jabbed a syringe filled with morphine through Lightfoot's fatigues and into his left thigh, then took out a pen and wrote the dose and time on the pant leg: 11:45 a.m.

At the landing zone, Dr. Jeffrey Millegan, the battalion medical officer, was struck by the contrast between the attention lavished on the wounded Marines, who were surrounded by friends, and the lonely suffering of the injured Iraqi, who had been left lying on the ground. Dr. Millegan, a Navy lieutenant, was something of an outsider himself at Camp Husaybah, and he felt trying to fit in with the grunts was akin to a naturalist trying to win the trust of a group of mountain gorillas. Millegan prided himself on being a return-them-to-duty doc, declining to order medevacs for Marines with minor wounds or ailments. Later he earned the grunts' enmity by shooting the feral black-and-white mutt that accompanied foot patrols through Husaybah and chased away the wild dogs that would otherwise bark and give away the Marine positions. With the dog as point man, the Marines could sometimes go through an entire patrol without a single dog barking. Dr. Millegan, a twenty-seven-year-old Oregonian, had figured it was just a matter of time before the dog bit someone, and he'd have to medevac the victim to a field hospital for rabies shots. He didn't want to risk a medevac helicopter crew or convoy over a dog bite. So he had lobbied for weeks for permission to kill the mutt and issued a standing offer to shoot him personally. But the dog had powerful friends around Camp Husaybah, until he became too territorial about his new home and attacked one of the aggressive German shepherds that the Marines used to sniff for bombs at the Syrian border. Dr. Millegan got the green light: when he found the mutt, he unholstered his pistol and shot him in the head. Afterward, the Navy Seabees picked up the dog's body with a fork lift and carried it through camp for burial, while angry Marines muttered about fragging the medical officer.

Dr. Millegan knew the Iraqi's injuries were far more serious than Lightfoot's or Roshak's, and, slipping his stethoscope into his ears, he could hear blood pooling in the man's lungs. The doctor sealed the wounds and rolled the Iraqi onto his right side. Blood poured out of the seals. Dr. Millegan ordered a corpsman to insert a tube in through the bullet wound in the Iraqi's chest, allowing blood to drain directly out of the lung as the Iraqi, Roshak, and Lightfoot flew off to al Qa'im in a Blackhawk helicopter ambulance.

While the Marines had initially been securing the Crackhouse, the sniper team, code-named Sierra Four, had been hunting for a good vantage point to provide cover fire for

Lieutenant Watson's patrols. If Marine infantrymen were trained to kill in the heat of battle, Marine scout snipers were trained to kill in cold blood. A sniper didn't bomb from above or fire artillery from afar. He wasn't supposed to engage in firefights at all. Instead, he was taught to move unseen behind enemy lines, look at his target through a powerful scope, calmly pull the trigger, and watch him fall. The biggest sniper rifles could rip open a man's torso or even penetrate a car's engine block from over a mile away. It was a very personal way to kill.

Not every Marine wanted such a job. Nor could every Marine pass the rigorous, three-month sniper course. Instructors demanded that their students be meticulously observant, since the smallest clue might reveal an enormous amount about the enemy. Discarded water bottles might give away the size of the enemy force. Food wrappers might betray weak morale or stretched supply lines. In one memory test for aspiring snipers, instructors placed ten items on the floor and gave the Marine one minute to examine them. The instructors shouted and threw things to distract the student, then covered the items up again. The Marine went about his daily work, exercising and studying. Hours later, the instructors gave him three minutes to draw each item and describe its size, shape, color, condition, and purpose. The Marine had to recall eight of the ten items accurately to pass. To pass stalking class, the student sniper had to creep unseen toward two instructors standing on a Humvee watching for his approach through binoculars. The student had to get within two hundred yards, fire two blank shots, and escape unnoticed. Advancing in exaggerated slow motion, the student stuffed leaves, grass, and sticks into his burlap suit to break up the outline of his body and rifle, changing his plant camouflage as he moved out of woodlands and into fields or back again. The best students concealed themselves so well that other Marines stepped on top of them without noticing.

But in a barren city such as Husaybah, where any Western face stood out, someone had to watch over the snipers while the snipers and their spotters watched for the enemy. So Lieutenant Watson sent four grunts, led by Lance Corporal Kurtis Bellmont, to provide security for Sierra Four as the team moved east from the Crackhouse to set up an observation post near the soccer field on East End. The bespectacled Bellmont was excited about the mission. He and his team were on their own, far from officers, sergeants, and the like, and the presence of the aloof snipers lent the assignment an air of mystery. Bellmont also had his own ideas about the safest way to set up an observation post. Most of all, he wanted to seize an occupied house. Husaybah was full of ornate concrete-block homes, only half-built, as if some real estate developer had gone bust in the middle of a subdivision. Such empty buildings were sometime booby-trapped, whereas insurgents generally wouldn't attack a house where other Iraqis lived. At the first house the Marines approached, however, they found only women at home. By local custom, it was taboo for strange men to enter an Iraqi house when none of the male residents were present. The Marines had been told they were supposed to win hearts and minds among the Iraqis, so they left in search of a more socially acceptable outpost.

Their cultural scruples went by the wayside, however, when they heard the bomb explode atop the Crackhouse, followed by bursts of rifle fire. There was chaotic chatter on the radio, and the snipers couldn't decipher what had happened or if anyone had been hurt. Corporal Steve Reifel, the sniper team's leader, immediately looked for a house with a view of the fighting. The Marines kicked in the steel gate of the nearest courtyard, and Bellmont and his men stood guard over the family that lived there while the snipers clambered upstairs. They found the view obstructed and pushed farther up the street to a three-story house under construction at the top of a rise, a little more than five hundred yards northeast of the Crackhouse. They discovered three masons at work in the house, more terrified than threatening, and corralled them into a ground-floor room before climbing to the roof.

The top of the staircase was enclosed by a hut, and the roof itself was rimmed with a foot-and-a-half-tall parapet. The two snipers and two spotters took off their flak jackets and helmets and crouched by the edge, scanning the surrounding rooftops and windows for muzzle flashes. The security team waited inside the hut, and Bellmont sat in the shade. The snipers saw nothing for about ten minutes, and the sound of gunfire from the Crackhouse died down.

Corporal Matt Thompson, one of the Sierra Four spotters, sat by the edge of the roof on his backpack. About noon, Thompson took a drink from his green plastic canteen and stood up with his scope to get a better view of the area. As he rose, he heard a single, very loud crack of a gunshot and felt a blow as if someone had taken a home-run swing at his upper legs. The slug punched into his left thigh from the outside, shattered his femur, exited between his legs, entered his right thigh, ripped through the muscle, exited again and mushroomed as it collided with the pistol hanging from his right hip. Thompson twisted as he fell, landing on his stomach and screaming in agony on the way down. He looked at his pants and saw blood seeping through the camouflage pattern. "I'm shot, I'm shot," he yelled. The other Marines had taken cover inside the hut, and Corporal Reifel didn't want them rushing out carelessly to help Thompson. He suspected the Iraqi sharpshooter—Marine snipers considered Iraqis unworthy of the title sniper—was waiting patiently for a chance to shoot the rescuer who came to Thompson's aid. The Marines realized to their chagrin that the team's radio was also out on the rooftop, so they couldn't even call for a medevac. Thompson, a twenty-one-year-old with the strong accent of his Gilmer, Texas, home, lay on his stomach facing the hut. He raised himself up on his elbows and shouted: "I'm hit in the legs."

Fifteen or twenty seconds passed, and then insurgents somewhere in the surrounding buildings loosed a series of sustained bursts of rifle fire at the rooftop. Lance Corporal Bellmont felt like everything suddenly slipped into slow motion, and Thompson's screams hit him in the gut. "Can you crawl?" he called from the hut.

"No," said Thompson. Thompson expected to be shot again at any moment and tried to brace himself to feel the excruciating pain in his legs repeated in some other part of his body.

"Lay down. Stay still," Reifel yelled to Thompson. "Keep your head down." Thompson did as he was told. Reifel saw blood smeared on the concrete and worried that the shot might have cut Thompson's femoral artery and that Thompson might bleed out right there on the roof. Lance Corporal Lucas Munds, who considered Thompson his best friend in the world, also felt time slow as he watched Thompson stare pleadingly at his friends. Finally the snipers couldn't stand it anymore. Munds dropped his M16 and snatched a light machine gun from one of the other Marines. Then he sprinted onto the roof, firing from the hip as he ran. At the edge he dropped to both knees and, with an uninterrupted squeeze of the trigger, sprayed the neighborhood with bullets. He saw no enemy fighters and had no idea where the round that had hit Thompson had come from, so he swept his muzzle from rooftop to doorway to window in the hope that the barrage would force the insurgents to stop firing. Corporal Reifel joined him with the M16 and fired off two thirty-round magazines, yelling at Munds—who in his hurry to protect Thompson had forgotten to take cover himself—to get behind the parapet.

From the staircase, Bellmont saw water squirting out of the holes that Munds and Reifel were shooting in the tanks on the building tops around them. The Iraqis' fire flagged, and Bellmont ran onto the open roof in a crouch. When he reached Thompson, he extended his hand. But Thompson kept his own hands clenched into fists and pulled tight to his chest underneath him. "Give me your hand," Bellmont said. Thompson didn't move. "Give me your hand," Bellmont repeated more emphatically, worried that at any moment he, too, might find himself writhing on the rooftop in pain. Thompson extended one arm, and the two men grasped each other's wrists as Bellmont dragged Thompson on his stomach into the hut, close rounds snapping overhead.

Inside, Bellmont pulled Thompson's pants down to his ankles and saw small chunks of muscle that had fallen away from his thighs. There was blood everywhere, but the wound wasn't spurting, so Bellmont knew the Iraqi had missed the artery. "Hey, man," Thompson said, trying to sound jocular so his buddies wouldn't think he was whining. "Make sure my dick's not shot off." Bellmont took a look and assured Thompson that everything was intact. Thompson's left thigh, however, was swollen to volleyball size, and the team had no corpsman or morphine to ease the searing pain. Bellmont wrapped Thompson's left leg, apologizing profusely as he lifted it to get the bandage underneath. Then he dressed the right leg.

With another Marine's help, Bellmont heaved Thompson onto his shoulder. "You're not going to fireman's-carry me down those stairs," Thompson screamed. But Bellmont said his only other choice was to have one Marine lift from the armpits while another lifted his legs. Thompson opted for the fireman's carry but bellowed with every bump on the way downstairs, his vision going black at times. "Put me down," Thompson ordered when they arrived at the front door.

"No, cuz it's going to hurt more to pick you back up again," Bellmont responded.

"Put me down or I'm going to throw up on you," Thompson said. Bellmont put him down.

Reifel and Munds had had their backs turned to Thompson as they fired and hadn't seen Bellmont pull the wounded man off the roof. When they paused after a minute or two of steady firing, they were surprised to see Thompson was no longer there. Growing up in Champaign, Illinois, Munds had given his parents so much trouble that a military academy seemed the only option; he liked it so much that he enlisted after graduation. Now the twenty-year-old realized he was kneeling in the open during the middle of a firefight, and for the first time envisioned himself getting shot. He dropped to his stomach, letting go of the front grip of the machine gun as he went down. The weapon was too heavy for him to steady with just one hand, and the muzzle tipped forward, firing wildly and sending concrete chips dancing across the rooftop. Munds released the trigger, and looked into the

gun's ammo drum. He had fired all but two or three of the
two hundred rounds it had held.

Munds grabbed Thompson's M16, and he and Reifel continued firing into the surrounding neighborhood, one duck-
ing down as the other one shot. Munds, the team's radio
operator, reached for the nearby handset and tried to remember proper procedure for calling in a medevac to the Lima
Company command post, using Thompson's call sign, Echo
Four Tango. "Lima CP this is Sierra Four requesting an urgent medevac," Munds said. "Echo Four Tango has been shot
through both his fucking legs." With the firefight still raging
at the Crackhouse, however, there were lots of voices on the
airwaves, and other Marines repeatedly cut in on Munds's
medevac call. Munds repeated the message four or five times,
and each time he got louder and more profane until he finally
just screamed: "Fucking Thompson is shot. We need a fucking urgent medevac right now."

Back at Lima's command post in Camp Husaybah, the
commander of the sniper platoon, First Lieutenant Doug
French, overheard the frantic radio traffic. He was frustrated
that his men were getting shot up and he was stuck in an office. But French, at twenty-five younger than some of his
Marines, knew that one thing he could do to give them a
chance of getting out alive was to dampen the chaos. He had
learned from his own company commander during the invasion of Iraq a year earlier to project an exaggerated calm over
the radio. He slowed his words and turned his voice into an
expressionless monotone. "You've gotta slow down," he said.
"You've gotta calm down. I need you to take that combat
pause and get us a grid so we can effect this medevac."

Munds felt a wave of confidence hit him when he heard
Lieutenant French's voice; it was like talking to a priest. He

took out his global positioning system and read off Sierra Four's coordinates. Somewhere along the way, however, the coordinates became scrambled, and the Humvees assigned the medevac mission ended up storming around Husaybah trying to find a wounded sniper. The snipers, still under sporadic fire, used every pyrotechnic in their packs—red starcluster fireworks, three-balled pop-up flares, yellow, green, and purple smoke grenades—to guide the medevac Humvees to the right spot. When the Humvees finally pulled up in front of the house the snipers were occupying, Corporal Reifel helped hoist Thompson back onto Bellmont's shoulder. "You'll be home in a week, seeing your fiancée and drinking a beer," Reifel told Thompson. He got a grin in return.

From the Crackhouse, Lieutenant Watson and his men swept through the neighborhood in search of insurgents and weapons caches. They found none. The Marines questioned the residents of a house where they had seen gunmen during the firefight. There were three women and several small children at home. The Marines found a couple of assault rifles and some shell casings on the steps. The women, however, denied having seen any insurgents or, for that matter, having noticed any gunfire at all in the neighborhood that day.

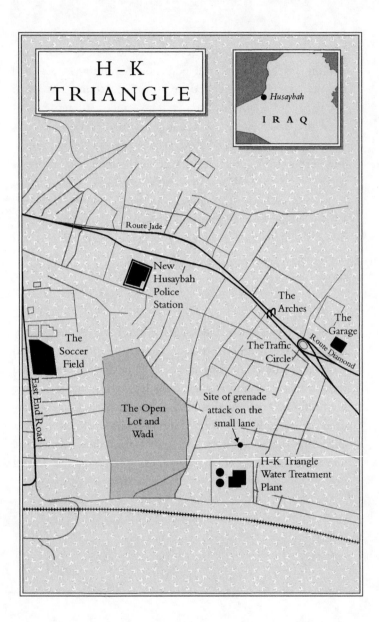

IV | *Convoy*

SERGEANT TOM HENDRICKS had a bad feeling about the April 14 convoy from the start. It wasn't so much the operation itself that worried him. It was a classic goodwill, nation-building, hearts-and-minds mission and wasn't supposed to involve any shooting. The battalion commander, Lieutenant Colonel Lopez, would take six Humvees and twenty-five or so Marines from their base in al Qa'im to the Karabilah police station, check out the renovations that the Marines had ordered, and deliver $70,000 in cash to the construction contractor if the job had been done right. At the same time, the colonel's convoy would link up with Corporal Dunham's squad to see if the police station would make a good base for Kilo Company. The colonel's convoy would then leave Dunham and his men in Karabilah, follow the Iraqi Police chief west to the new Husaybah station house, and conduct a spot check to see if the U.S.-funded cops there were doing any actual policing. Most of the Iraqi Police officers had been cops under Saddam, and the Marines had just put them through a reeducation academy in the hopes they would take on more of the fight against the insurgency.

What troubled Sergeant Hendricks about the plan was that so many Iraqis knew the convoy was coming. He figured if the police knew the Marines were paying a visit, someone would tip off the insurgents as well. For all he knew, the police were the insurgents. The twenty-four-year-old sergeant had wanted to be a Marine since he was in the ninth grade in New Jersey. His grandfather had worn the uniform at Guadalcanal, and Hendricks remembered seeing him shaken whenever he heard the sound of police or fire sirens. Only after Hendricks joined the Marines did his grandfather start sharing war stories. The night before the convoy to Karabilah, Hendricks found himself edgy as well. "Almost guaranteed action," he wrote in his journal. "Well, if this is my last entry because we get hit . . . it's been fun. Goodnight."

Karabilah was a narrow strip of houses and farmland just east of Husaybah. Two main roads ran roughly east–west and roughly parallel through Karabilah. Since the Marines didn't know most of the Arabic street names and preferred code words anyway, they called the southern road Route Jade and the northern one Route Diamond. When the Army had occupied the border area, the soldiers had named the roads after porn magazines—Route Playboy, Route Penthouse, Route Hustler, Route Cheri, and the like. The Marines, seeking to convey a more culturally sensitive image in Muslim Iraq, changed the road names to gemstones and minerals, and named the helicopter landing zones after birds, including LZ Dodo, LZ Sparrow, LZ Wren, and LZ Crow.

As Jade and Diamond approached Husaybah, Jade angled

more sharply to the northwest until the two roads merged at a traffic circle. In the Marines' satellite reconnaissance photos the circle resembled the shape of the looped yellow ribbons that adorned their families' cars and mailboxes back home. After the circle the road, now just called Jade, passed under a pair of shabby, side-by-side monumental arches that the Army troops called the McDonald's arches. Between them was a billboard that at one time had held portraits of Saddam Hussein. On the way into Husaybah he had appeared in traditional Arab robe and headdress. On the way out he had been in his military uniform. The portraits were torn down after his regime fell. South of the arches lay a large, wedge-shaped neighborhood that the Marines, unsure whether it belonged to Husaybah or Karabilah, called the H-K Triangle. West of the arches, the lanes of Jade split around each side of the cemetery on the median strip, passed the Husaybah police station, and then joined again to form Market Street, the store-lined road that ran straight west along the city's northern side and ended at Camp Husaybah and the Syrian border.

While Lieutenant Colonel Lopez talked with the police chief, Corporal Dunham's patrol cased the Karabilah police station to see if it could comfortably house Kilo Company and enable the Marines to saturate the town with joint U.S.-Iraqi foot patrols. Most of the grunts didn't know it, but the mission had its roots in the Vietnam War. Not much made U.S. commanders in Iraq edgier than comparisons with Vietnam. The notion that the occupation of Iraq might devolve into a quagmire, that Iraqi hearts and minds could not be won or even subdued, sent shivers of indignation down military spines. But the Marines felt there were lessons they had learned in the jungles of Vietnam that might hold in the

desert, too. One of those was the notion that, in very compact areas, a small unit of infantrymen could make headway
against a guerrilla force by living and fighting alongside the
locals. In Vietnam, a small number of Marine squads set up
camp inside villages that were heavily infiltrated by the Viet-
cong. During the day they socialized with the residents,
drinking beer and sharing food. At night they patrolled the
rice paddies and pathways, hunting for guerrillas and dodging
ambushes. Marine casualties were very high. But they gradually won the trust of war-weary civilians and the assistance of
the South Vietnamese security forces.

In the hostile towns of western Iraq, the Marines cus-
tomized the village experiments of Indochina by placing
slightly larger units—a platoon or more—in local police stations. Joint patrols and raids, the theory went, would buck
up Iraqi Police and Civil Defense Corps troops and show
civilians that the Marines wouldn't abandon them to face
insurgent violence alone. The experiment was plagued by
setbacks. The Marines were never quite sure which Iraqi security men were on their side and which were against them,
and even those who seemed friendly often refused to patrol
with the Americans for fear of insurgent reprisals. Despite the
headaches, though, Marine commanders saw the Iraqi security forces as their best hope for stabilizing the region and going home.

Corporal Dunham arrayed his men around the station to
watch for surprise attacks while Captain Gibson, Kilo Company's commander, Gunnery Sergeant Elia Fontecchio, one
of the company's senior enlisted men, and Staff Sergeant
Ferguson of Fourth Platoon inspected the station house. Pfc.
Miller, the boot, and Lance Corporal Hampton, the fire-
team leader, stood guard together at the school next door,

where Iraqi children gathered around asking for money. The crowd made Hampton edgy. He'd heard a story about an Army soldier gunned down at close range in Husaybah while distracted by a group of civilians. So Hampton borrowed a dollar bill from Miller and picked a big teenager out of the crowd. Then he grabbed another boy, shook him, and pushed him away. He held Miller's dollar in front of the big teen and explained, through hand gestures, that he could keep the money if he chased away the other children in similar fashion. The teen dutifully thumped the others.

The colonel's convoy left Dunham's patrol behind at the Karabilah police station around noon, and followed the Iraqi Police chief in his squad car. Initially the convoy commander, Major Ezra Carbins, had told the police chief to lead the Marines north from the Karabilah station house to take Route Diamond into Husaybah, about a mile and a half away. But there were rumors that the police chief was in cahoots with the insurgents, and Major Carbins and Lieutenant Colonel Lopez were wary of a trap. Already the convoy had received radio reports about the bomb at the Crackhouse that morning. So at the last moment the major pulled the police chief aside and instructed him to take the southern road, Jade, into Husaybah instead.

Major Carbins, a mild-tempered thirty-three-year-old, had been in Oakland conducting undercover investigations for the Drug Enforcement Administration when his reserve unit was called up for active duty. As invasion had turned to occupation, the Pentagon had grown heavily dependent on reservists and National Guardsmen with specialized expertise—business executives, lawyers, police officers, and the like—to try to build the institutions of a new Iraqi society. Major Carbins's detachment, code-named Peacemaker, was just such a civil-affairs unit. But he found himself short of specialists and made do with what he had. Sergeant Hendricks's civilian job was as a physical trainer at the gym at a Marine base. He'd help less athletic Marines pass their fitness tests, help injured Marines recover, and help fat Marines lose weight. Major Carbins considered him a go-getter and appointed him liaison to the director of the al Qa'im phosphate plant, one of the main hopes for economic growth in the area. Hendricks hoped to tap the Internet to drum up customers for the plant's fertilizer. Staff Sergeant Joe Mallicoat owned an archery shop back in Vancouver, Washington, so Carbins made him project manager dealing with the Iraqi contractors the Marines hired to fix the water supply, repair the sewage system, and clean up the streets. The major tapped Captain Kyle Lewis, the battalion judge advocate, to handle financial claims from Iraqis who felt the Marines had wrongly destroyed their property or killed their relatives. As a cop, Carbins's main duty was to ensure the local police and civil defense troops were trained and cleansed of rebel sympathies so the Marines could take on a lower profile, suffer fewer casualties, and eventually leave the country entirely.

Major Carbins rode in a heavily armored green Humvee built to resist bombs, mines, and bullets, with the other five less armored Humvees strung out behind him. The vehicles followed the Iraqi police chief's squad car at fifty-yard intervals so that a mine or bomb would only destroy one at a time. Major Carbins sat next to his driver, Corporal Christopher Golden, a thirty-five-year-old diesel mechanic from Alabama. Staff Sergeant Mallicoat rode behind Golden and Pfc. Kyle Stilling stood up in the turret manning the machine gun.

The first signs of trouble were the green and red star clusters that suddenly rose into the sky ahead as the convoy drove west on Jade. U.S. intelligence reports suggested that the insurgents—whom Marines and locals alike called the Mujahedeen—used fireworks as a signaling system, and Major Carbins thought the colorful display up ahead might be a signal that his own convoy was on its way into an ambush. As the Humvees headed toward the traffic circle, Corporal Golden saw a group of Iraqi men scatter in a parking lot off the right side of the road. Moments later, the Marines saw a flash off the right side of the road, in front of a mechanic's shop well ahead of their position. A deep boom and a plume of gray smoke instantly followed.

Within seconds the convoy entered the kill zone of a well-laid ambush and broke up under a barrage of fire.

———————

Typically every fifth round in a machine-gun ammunition belt is an illuminated tracer that burns red or green as it flies through the air to help the gunner steer his fire toward his target. It's a two-way street, however. Tracers also allow the people being shot at to track the line backward and figure out where the attack is coming from. As Major Carbins's Humvee approached the traffic circle, the Marines inside saw a line of red tracers whip by and knew the gunner was in a small building next to a mosque on the left side of Jade. Gunmen wearing red-and-white-checkered scarves over their faces appeared in the windows of several low, mud-brick buildings, the muzzles of their rifles flashing as they poured fire into the passing convoy. Golden and Mallicoat turned their heads toward the source of the gunfire in time to see the thick bulletproof glass in their windows crack in a spiderweb pattern as they were hit by machine-gun rounds. Laden with heavy combat gear, Mallicoat was trying to twist into a position to look back down Jade, and his face and helmet were touching the glass when the round hit. He caught an acrid scent of molten lead penetrating the vehicle as the bullet disintegrated. *I'm still alive,* he thought in amazement.

Golden and Mallicoat yelled that the attackers were to their left, only to have another group of ambushers loose a volley of rifle fire from the right side of the road. Bullets ricocheted off the Humvee's armored exterior. Pfc. Stilling, the turret gunner, protruded through a hole in the Humvee's roof, however, and had little armor to protect him. Stilling was a hulking, blond twenty-year-old who grew up hunting duck near the Puget Sound. Gripping his 240-G medium machine gun, he found himself tangled in ropes of red tracer fire coming from the roadside behind him. Before he could swing around and return fire, an Iraqi slug hit the feed-tray cover that clicked down over the ammunition belt on his weapon. The impact set off one of the rounds inside Stilling's gun, with a bang that sounded like a firecracker. Stilling knew immediately that his machine gun, the Humvee's main defense, was useless. He bent over and shouted through the round opening in the roof: "My 240's down."

Corporal Golden kept one hand on the wheel, reached back with the other, and pulled Stilling into the vehicle. "Well then get down," he yelled. Stilling squatted low to get his head out of the crossfire.

As a swarm of RPGs—rocket-propelled grenades—zipped by overhead, Major Carbins told Golden to pull over fifty yards farther up Jade. The major wanted to set up a firing position to protect the five more-vulnerable Humvees as they ran the Iraqi gauntlet. "Staff Sergeant, let's go," Carbins said

to Mallicoat. "Let's get out." The major reminded himself to
stay calm. But another voice inside questioned the wisdom of
getting out of an armored vehicle in the middle of an ambush. Iraqi rifle rounds were pounding the Humvee, and the
major couldn't see anyone to shoot back at. Carbins had
drawn his weapon on several drug busts in Oakland, but
none of the dealers had ever taken a shot at him. *This is crazy,*
he said to himself. Then he opened the door and ran for the
north side of Jade.

Staff Sergeant Mallicoat, getting his first taste of combat,
wanted to get out of the Humvee as fast as possible. The armor had held up well against machine-gun fire, but he had
no idea whether it would withstand an RPG shot. The RPG,
fired from the shoulder like a bazooka, was the great equal-
izer in Third World urban combat. One malnourished insurgent in blue jeans and a T-shirt could pop around a corner,
get off a lucky RPG shot, and kill a lot of expensively
equipped American troops. RPGs had downed two Blackhawk helicopters in Somalia in 1993. Mallicoat thought the
armored Humvee might survive a glancing RPG blow, but
he doubted it could take a direct hit in the side. He had no
intention of waiting inside to find out, and he quickly joined
Major Carbins north of the road.

Lieutenant Colonel Matt Lopez's Humvee was third in line
in the convoy. A battalion commander at age forty, Lopez
found himself ruling a broad swath of Iraq like a colonial po-
tentate. He could dictate who sat on city councils, who ran
the police department, who got how much American money
for what project. He could have men arrested. He could get
them released. He did all those things at one time or another,

depending on whether he thought it would buy some peace and prosperity for the cities, towns, and desert wastelands his men occupied. More than anything, however, he loved being able to stop his Humvee on the street and hand out a piece of candy, a stuffed bear, or a new soccer ball to some impoverished Iraqi child. His sympathy for waifs was inherited; when Matt was growing up back in Chicago, his own mother had taken in any number of foster children, caring for them for a few days or even a few years until they could find stable homes. Lopez felt equally paternal toward his own Marines. He never asked them to take risks that he didn't take himself, and he refused to commandeer one of the prized armored Humvees that stopped bullets and blunted blasts. His vehicle just had some Kevlar blankets and steel plates under the seats, and improvised, thin steel doors that left the passengers' heads exposed to fire.

The colonel's seeming disregard for his own safety drove his bodyguard and translator, Lance Corporal Akram Falah, to distraction. Falah wore his hair in a strip down the center of his scalp, with the sides shaved close, a traditional Marine cut called a high-and-tight. The style emphasized his long nose, prominent ears, and lively brown eyes. Falah had been born in Kuwait of Palestinian parents who moved to Anaheim, California, and he hoped his military service would help him turn his green card into U.S. citizenship. Falah's family had fallen apart in their new homeland, and he didn't tell either parent that he had converted from Islam to Christianity shortly before the battalion went back to Iraq. Instead he found fathers and brothers among the Marines. First among them was the colonel himself, who relied heavily on Falah's linguistic skills to cajole cooperation from the local sheik or decipher the incendiary rhetoric blasting from the mosques. Falah, however, believed his real mission was to get Lieutenant Colonel Lopez home safely to his family and believed the biggest obstacle to making that happen was the colonel himself. On more than one occasion, Falah had seen Lopez kick a bag or pile of trash on the side of the road, ideal hiding places for bombs. But the colonel was the colonel, and Falah followed along in loyal silence.

When the convoy tripped the ambush, Lance Corporal Darren Pickard, the colonel's driver, heard the explosion by the mechanic's shop up the road and saw heads appear in the windows, doorways, and breaks in the walls that lined the south side of Jade. Iraqis peeked around corners, fired off a few shots with their assault rifles, and then ducked out of view. Steering with his knee at thirty-five miles per hour, Pickard fired his M16 rifle at an Iraqi fighter in a ground-floor window but couldn't tell whether he hit the man. He heard the ping of bullets against the Humvee and watched his side rear-view mirror evaporate. The colonel, sitting behind Pickard, saw at least a dozen RPGs crisscross overhead in the first ten seconds of the ambush, while machine-gun tracers skimmed over the Humvee's hood. Lopez opened fire with his M4 rifle, a stubby version of the M16 that was easier to maneuver in tight spaces. One Iraqi round went through the plywood that covered the flat area next to the colonel's seat and narrowly missed the colonel's head as he leaned out to shoot.

Lance Corporal Falah, in the front passenger seat, pulled his right leg up, sat on his ankle, and aimed his rifle through the gap in the steel-plate door. He wanted as wide a field of fire as he could get to cover the Humvee's right side. Falah heard the colonel and Pickard yell, "Contact!" but he couldn't see any Iraqis to shoot on his side of the vehicle. He heard rounds snapping by his head as they flew in through the left-side windows and out through the right, and an instant later he felt as if his left arm had burst into flames. Falah erupted in a series of anguished, animal screams. "Motherfuckers," he yelled. "I'm hit, I'm hit." The bullet had come from behind Falah, drilled through the butt of his rifle, pierced his left biceps, shredded the nerves, severed the brachial artery that carried blood from his heart to his fingers, and exited the other side, exposing a ghastly pulp of pulverized muscle and blood. Pickard, the driver, looked to his right and saw a fountain of blood pulsate out of Falah's upper arm with every beat of his heart. Half-dollar-sized chunks of Falah's flesh fell to the Humvee floor.

Moments later, between RPG volleys, another rifle round hit the vehicle from behind. This one penetrated the left-rear wheel well behind Lopez, zigged upward, slid under the colonel's flak vest, and cut a gouge into the right side of his back. The colonel didn't mention it to the others.

Pickard turned back to the driver's window and looked for the Iraqi he had been shooting at seconds earlier. The man was gone, so Pickard squeezed off some rounds at other ambushers before he spotted a head wrapped in a red-and-white-checkered scarf bobbing behind a chin-high wall some seventy-five yards ahead. The man disappeared briefly, then appeared over the wall again, this time with the slender silhouette of an RPG launcher visible on his shoulder. The angle was such that the man had a clear shot at the colonel's Humvee, but the windshield frame and steel door plating prevented Pickard from positioning his rifle to shoot back. *Oh, shit,* Pickard said to himself. He veered right and stepped down on the gas pedal. The grenade tore the air with a buzzing crescendo as Pickard swerved, hitting the rubberized tan tarpaulin and metal support frame on the Humvee's rear bed and passing through unexploded. It detonated when it hit a building on the far side of Jade.

Falah kept up a steady agonal scream until the Humvee passed the traffic circle and reached the arches. He banged his head on the steel door to try to kill the pain, looked down at the blood drenching his uniform and coating the floor of the Humvee, and slumped forward, his forehead resting where the dashboard met the door. Pickard saw the back of Falah's head painted in blood and figured he was probably dead. "Get out of here," Lopez instructed Pickard. "Go-go-go." The colonel ordered him to drive straight to Camp Husaybah, just over two miles away. Lopez assumed the rest of the convoy would follow along, but, at the moment, he just wanted to get Falah to a corpsman before he bled to death. The colonel had heard on the radio that medevac helicopters were inbound for Lima Company's camp to pick up the Crackhouse casualties, and he could see two helos flying over the city to his left. Pickard stormed down Market Street at sixty-five miles per hour, slaloming past appliance shops, grocery stores, and three-wheeled motorized carts. He steered with his left hand and kept the other pressed to the horn. The Humvee skidded to a stop at LZ Parrot. Pickard jumped out yelling: "We got a casualty. Falah has been hit."

A corpsman pulled Falah onto the ground, cut off his sleeve and poured a powder called QuikClot onto the gash on his left arm. QuickClot was a new commercial clotting agent that had just been put into widespread military use for the invasion of Iraq. The trauma doctors already considered it a lifesaver in the field because it almost instantly sealed off even major wounds. The powder, however, felt like a red-hot cattle brand to the wounded man.

Falah was pretty sure that while he was unconscious, he saw Jesus. He remembered seeing a lot of light, a body and hair, but no face. He felt Jesus touch his hand and pull him upward, then set him down again. Falah felt Jesus stroke his face. As the QuikClot hit his wound, Falah regained consciousness and screamed again, directing his rage at the Iraqis. "You fucking rag heads," he bellowed. "You fucking camel jockeys." The corpsman gave him morphine. The QuickClot slowed the bleeding, but didn't stop it. A first-aid tourniquet also failed to stem the flow, and finally the docs improvised with a tourniquet made from a stick and strips of Falah's uniform.

One of the gunnery sergeants tried to calm Falah down. "Does America love me, Gunny?" Falah asked him. "Does America love me?"

"Yes—America loves you," the gunny assured Falah.

Pickard paced in circles, addled with adrenalin, until he noticed that Lieutenant Colonel Lopez was still sitting in the Humvee. The colonel leaned his head back against the seat, his eyes staring straight ahead, his rifle in his hands. He turned to meet Pickard's gaze. "Sir? Are you all right?" Pickard asked.

"I've been hit," Lopez responded. "On my right side."

Pickard opened the door and leaned across the colonel's lap. "Sir, I don't see any blood."

"I know—I was just scraped," Lopez said.

Pickard went back to the other side of the Humvee, where Falah was rambling on about getting back to the firefight. As the Army medic prepared to load him onto the Blackhawk, Falah grabbed her, lifted himself up off the stretcher and kissed the American flag patch on her sleeve. "Take care of my colonel," he yelled as he was carried away.

The six-vehicle convoy had unintentionally split in half when Lopez decided to rush Falah to the landing zone; just two other Humvees followed him through Husaybah. One was the fifth vehicle in line, which carried only a corpsman and a driver. The other was the fourth Humvee, which carried Lopez's lawyer, Captain Lewis. The battalion hadn't held any courts martial in Iraq, but Captain Lewis had other duties to keep him busy. He helped negotiate disputes with the Syrians and assisted the nascent Iraqi border authorities with implementation of U.S.-imposed duty and customs laws. He also dealt with the touchy issue of caring for the many Iraqis the Marines detained for suspected anticoalition activities, and he tried to inject momentum into the stagnant Iraqi criminal justice system, which hadn't prosecuted anyone in Husaybah for more than six months. Lieutenant Colonel Lopez wanted Captain Lewis along on the convoy to scope out possible sites for a new city jail.

Captain Lewis had borrowed a driver, whose name he never quite caught, and put a nineteen-year-old private first class, John Simental, in the turret manning the machine gun. Simental was a math student at Cal State Long Beach and had joined the Marine Corps Reserve expecting to do weekend-warrior duty until he graduated and landed a job teaching high school. Two combat engineers were supposed to be sitting in the back seats, but they hadn't shown up by the time the convoy left al Qa'im.

The first Iraqi machine-gun rounds passed over Captain Lewis's vehicle. The next volley poured in from the front left and made a thwacking sound as the rounds hit the Humvee's body, like a wooden spatula hitting a table. Simental reached down and released the locking device to allow the turret to rotate. As he started to turn his machine gun toward where he thought the attackers might be, an Iraqi round snapped through the Humvee's door, sending a metal door fragment deep into his right calf, where it settled about an inch from the bone. At first the pain from the blow stunned him, and he dropped down out of the turret. Soon, however, his leg went numb. Captain Lewis looked back over his shoulder at Simental, tapped him on the head and told him to get back up on the gun. As Simental stood up, Lewis saw the left rear window break and bullets tear into the radio and dashboard in an explosion of violence that reminded him of a swarm of angry bees. The rounds ripped through the rear seat, where one of the truant engineers was supposed to be sitting. Lewis felt a punch to the back of his left arm, and noticed something brush by his left side. He looked down at his left pant leg and saw the fabric suddenly buckle.

Simental had been shot before he could lock the turret into place, and as the Humvee careened through the ambush, the turret swung wildly from side to side. Soon he found himself down in the passenger compartment again. Captain Lewis was anxious to report Simental's injury and at first didn't realize that he, too, had been shot. The radio handset produced only static, however, and as the Humvee gunned it through the arches, Lewis looked at his left arm and saw bright red soaking through his sleeve and dripping onto the console that separated his seat from the driver's seat. He reached for the plastic medical kit strapped to the front of his vest. He pulled it open, scattering a handful of Advil pills around the cabin. A bullet had hit his first-aid kit and broken the Advil bottle, which struck him as quite funny even as he ripped open a bandage with his teeth and tried to wrap his left arm with his right hand. Simental squatted on the center console between the two seats, resting his own injured leg in the rear passenger foot well. He leaned forward to help Lewis wrap his arm. Simental's hand and knees were wet with the captain's blood as he pressed down on the bandage to contain the leakage.

Captain Lewis thought he should head back into the fight, but he had no radio contact and had lost sight of the colonel's vehicle as well as the three Humvees that had stayed back in the area of the ambush. So his driver raced on to Camp Husaybah. Lewis got out of the Humvee and saw the blood that had collected at his feet. Simental and the corpsman steadied the captain as he staggered through camp, his vision narrowing until he saw only a tunnel of light. He lay down in the shade outside the chow hall.

Lewis had been shot three times. One bullet had skimmed his left leg, gouging out a divot the size of a walnut about three inches above the kneecap. The wound never bled and left a slight burn mark, so the captain figured later it was probably a tracer round that both caused the wound and cauterized it at the same time. A second bullet had brushed by the side of his knee, but Lewis didn't realize it until a doctor pointed the scrape out to him a week later.

The third bullet had entered his left triceps, narrowly missed the bone, nicked the vital brachial artery, slashed through his biceps, and come to a stop inside his arm. Lewis saw the point of the bullet poking out of his skin and worried that it might catch on his uniform. So he pushed the slug all the way back in. Later the captain got to his feet to hitch a short ride to LZ Parrot. He turned back and saw a pool of blood on the spot where he had been lying. The sight angered him. He didn't want to make a mess in a fellow captain's camp, and he didn't want the grunts to have to walk by another Marine's blood. He ordered some corpsmen to get jugs of water and wash the stain away.

———————

Back on Jade, Sergeant Hendricks, who had had the gloomy premonition about the day's mission, saw Major Carbins pull over to the side of the road to protect the rest of the convoy. As Hendricks roared past, an Iraqi round hit his Humvee, the second in line, from behind and pierced the rubberized cover that stretched over the rear bed. The bullet flew into the passenger cabin, passed through the backpack canteen of the man riding in the left rear seat, then angled across Hendricks's left arm, missing his flesh but ripping through the flap and button on his sleeve pocket. The round exited through the windshield and drilled a plum-sized hole in the exhaust pipe that jutted up from the hood.

"Did I call it or what?" he wrote in his journal that night. "We drove right into the kill zone." Hendricks and his crew pulled over and watched the colonel, Captain Lewis, and the other Humvee race away toward the landing zone. Then they took up a position blocking traffic near the arches.

———————

Lance Corporal Rob Whittenberg was the turret gunner in the last Humvee in the convoy. A polite, open-faced twenty-two-year-old with big hands, Whittenberg had a map of Texas tattooed on his chest, with the red, white, and blue state flag inside and a caption that read "Deep in the Heart." Whittenberg's commanding officers sat at his feet, Second

Lieutenant Ryan Gordinier in the back and Captain Brad Tippett in the front. Next to Gordinier sat an Iraqi translator, Ayad. The gun truck had antishrapnel windows and fiberglass doors but nothing hard enough to stop a rifle shot. Whittenberg heard an RPG zoom by a few feet over his head, followed by a long burst of machine-gun fire. Ayad had refused the heavy bulletproof vest the Marines had offered him before leaving the base at al Qa'im, and one of the first rounds to hit the Humvee penetrated the rear panel of the vehicle and lodged inside his lower back. Lieutenant Gordinier yelled to the others, "Ayad's shot. He's looking pretty bad." He reached behind Whittenberg's legs and pressed both hands against Ayad's wound to contain the bleeding.

Captain Tippett looked back at Ayad just as an RPG hit outside the left side of the Humvee. Shrapnel sent cracks running through Ayad's window and peppered the vehicle's body. Fiberglass fragments hit Tippett in the face and goggles. The captain barked instructions up to Whittenberg, who was facing backward with the machine gun to protect the rear of the convoy. "Gun left," Tippett yelled to get Whittenberg to rotate the turret to cover the south side of the road.

Whittenberg leaned down from the turret. "We're taking fire, sir," he said to Lieutenant Gordinier.

"O.K., Whittenberg, where's it coming from?" the lieutenant asked.

"The front, sir."

"The front where?"

"The front right, sir."

The lieutenant couldn't hide his irritation. "Well, shoot," he said.

Whittenberg stood back up and started looking for something to fire his gun at, but he didn't see anyone who looked like the enemy. He shot off a couple of short bursts and thought he might have hit a car coming down the wrong side of the road. He shot at a building to his right. Then, hearing the lieutenant's voice again, he bent down to listen. As he leaned over, he felt a sharp pain in his right hip. The steel jacket of an Iraqi bullet had penetrated Whittenberg's aluminum canteen cup, poked a hole through his plastic canteen, and punched into his buttock, leaving the lead core of the round lodged inside the canteen itself. "I've been hit, sir," he said to the lieutenant.

Gordinier saw water pouring out of Whittenberg's canteen. "It's your canteen, it's your canteen," the lieutenant assured him. "Stand up and fire."

Whittenberg stood back up, and fired a burst or two at another building before the Humvee pulled out of the far side of the ambush area. Captain Tippett was furious with Whittenberg for coming down out of the turret and later discussed charging him with dereliction of duty. In an ambush, the machine gun was supposed to provide suppressing fire, a barrage so fierce that the ambushers would take cover and stop firing. Whittenberg, for his part, never saw any Iraqi fighters and didn't know whom he was supposed to kill. U.S. rules of engagement, designed to minimize the killing of civilians and alienation of the Iraqi public, required American troops to make a positive identification of the enemy before firing.

Lieutenant Gordinier had more sympathy for Whittenberg than did Captain Tippett. Whittenberg was trained as a rifleman, not a turret gunner, and the lieutenant had taken pains before the convoy left to explain that commands like "gun left" and "gun right" referred to the direction the vehicle was facing, which might be confusing to a turret gunner facing backward. Besides, the lieutenant never saw an enemy fighter during the ambush either.

Captain Tippett's Humvee raced to the traffic circle and pulled over near the arches to block traffic heading back toward the ambush site. Lieutenant Gordinier wrapped a bandage around Ayad's chest under his shirt. The other Marines spotted blood on Whittenberg's trousers and realized that he had indeed been shot, just not badly enough to require urgent care. Ayad, a forty-something contract hire from Baghdad, wanted nothing to do with the Marines at that point. Despite his wound, he stepped out of the Humvee, walked to a nearby courtyard and lit a cigarette. Captain Tippett saw Cobra attack helicopters overhead but couldn't raise them on the radio. He had no idea where Lieutenant Colonel Lopez's vehicle had gone, or the other two missing Humvees. Nor could he reach Major Carbins's Humvee, which was still somewhere behind him on Jade.

After Major Carbins had pulled over to the right side of the road to provide covering fire for the rest of the convoy, Pfc. Stilling, the major's turret gunner, watched the colonel, Captain Lewis, and the other Humvee speed away from the ambush and disappear toward Husaybah. Sergeant Hendricks's and Captain Tippett's Humvees blew by and parked far up ahead, near the McDonald's arches. Major Carbins and Staff Sergeant Mallicoat had left on foot to look for insurgents. Corporal Golden had stepped out and taken cover behind the driver's door, spraying bursts down Jade to try to keep the Iraqi machine gun quiet. Stilling realized he was the only man left in the only vehicle still in the kill zone, and his machine gun, hit by an Iraqi bullet, was useless. So he fished an M16 out of the

Humvee and stood back up in the turret, keyed the radio handset, and tried to call battalion headquarters to send out the quick-reaction force. He felt his heart pumping so fast that everything happening around him seemed in slow motion by comparison, until Golden screamed, "RPG."

The shooter wore a white robe that the Marines called a man-dress and a red-and-white kaffiyeh scarf that exposed only his eyes. He stood behind a chest-high wall on Jade, with a good angle for a kill shot on the Humvee's rear end. He fired too low, however, or perhaps the grenade was defective. Golden and Stilling stared in amazement as the warhead scraped against the surface of the road and skipped cartoonishly past the Humvee with a metallic *ting-ting* sound. It bounced all the way to the arches, where it ground to a halt in the middle of the street, unexploded.

After it passed, Golden turned back to look for the man with the RPG and spotted him near a big blue sedan, crouching down for cover and loading another pointed projectile into the launch tube. Golden aimed his M16 and, as the Iraqi lifted the launcher back onto his shoulder, let loose a burst. The Iraqi jerked backward, and the launcher tipped over as his arms flew up in the air. A few other Iraqi men pulled him into the sedan, took a right turn, and sped away on Jade. Golden pumped a few shots into the car and saw the impacts kick up a cloud of paint chips and glass.

Golden picked up Carbins and Mallicoat, and more RPG and machine-gun fire chased them toward the arches, where Captain Tippett and Sergeant Hendricks were waiting. Major Carbins told Golden to keep driving the short distance to the new Husaybah police station, which they had been planning to visit with the convoy. The Iraqi Police officers came out carrying their AKs and pistols upside down by their trigger guards in a sign of surrender. "Thanks for the help, ass-holes," Pfc. Stilling said loudly. Major Carbins grabbed the police chief who had led them through the ambush and ordered him to search the neighborhoods and fields north of Jade. The major noticed bitterly that the police chief's squad car was unscathed.

The entire ambush had lasted just a few minutes.

From the arches the Marines could see back down Diamond and, a few hundred yards distant, they watched Corporal Dunham's Kilo Company patrol clamber out of their vehicles and head into the H–K Triangle. Pfc. Stilling, the turret gunner, mistakenly believed the patrol was the quick-reaction force he had requested. *Go get those motherfuckers,* he said to himself.

Captain Tippett had a darker thought. What if Dunham and his men didn't know they were walking into the kill zone? He considered mounting up and trying to intercept Dunham's patrol, but feared that if they didn't plan it out first, Marines might end up shooting at each other in the confusion of battle. The captain tried for several minutes to radio a warning: "Any Kilo unit in the vicinity of the arches."

He got no response.

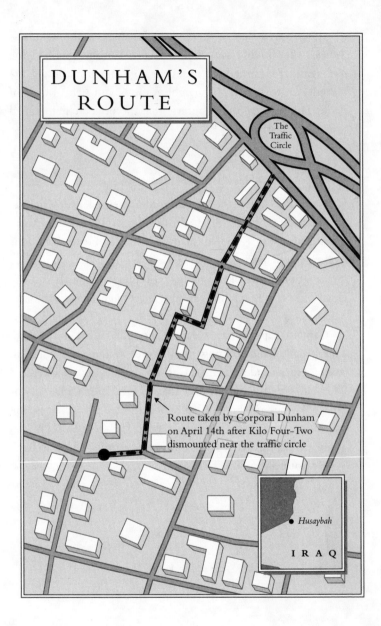

DUNHAM'S
ROUTE

The
Traffic
Circle

Route taken by Corporal Dunham
on April 14th after Kilo Four-Two
dismounted near the traffic circle

Husaybah

IRAQ

v | Kilo Four–Two

H-K Triangle, Iraq

BACK AT THE Karabilah police station, a sense of foreboding had settled over Corporal Dunham's patrol, Kilo Four-Two, within minutes of the convoy's departure. The Iraqi children who had been such pests to Lance Corporal Hampton and Pfc. Miller, begging for money and candy, suddenly melted away into the neighborhood. Sketchy radio reports started coming in about some Marine unit somewhere coming under fire. Captain Gibson heard what sounded like the thud of mortars being launched several hundred yards to the west. Miller caught the rattle of machine guns from the direction of the arches. Captain Gibson turned to Dunham. "What do you think?" he asked. Dunham said he thought the Iraqis were hitting Lima Company with mortars at Camp Husaybah.

"Well," Gibson said, "let's go get those fuckers."

Dunham rallied his men with shouts of "Let's *go*," and the patrol split into staggered columns and walked cautiously along the edges of the road toward the sound of firing. Captain Gibson—Captain America to the men of Kilo Company—found the slow pace exasperating. "What the hell are you doing?" he demanded. "Our brothers are getting into a fight. What are you doing walking?" The squad broke into a run and sprinted four hundred yards north to Route Diamond.

As he ran, Miller realized he might soon face that test of courage he had sought when he wandered into the Marine Corps recruiting office in the strip mall in Eureka. His first thought was whether he should take his M16 off its safe setting now or wait until he saw somebody to shoot at. Hampton, his fire-team leader, told him to leave the safety on. If he got into a fight, it just took a flick of the thumb to switch the weapon off safe and be ready to fire a shot with each squeeze of the trigger. But if he set the rifle to fire right away, he risked shooting off a round by accident while running. Such negligent discharges were heavily penalized by the Marines, largely because the most likely victims of errant shots were other Marines.

Lance Corporal Jason Sanders, the radio operator, had no intention of sprinting a mile and a half into Husaybah, so he called ahead to get the Humvees to meet them on Route Diamond. The squad climbed into the high-back Humvees and, as they raced northwest on Diamond toward the arches, Captain Gibson overheard radio traffic about the ambush of the colonel's convoy up ahead. It hadn't been mortars he and Dunham had heard after all. In the bed of one of the highbacks, Staff Sergeant Ferguson, the platoon's top enlisted man, reminded Dunham to assign each of his Marines a sector of fire, so they'd have guns pointing in every direction. "They will not get an RPG off on us," Ferguson said.

Moments later, just east of the traffic circle where Diamond met Jade, the Marines heard the whiz of an RPG cutting across their path from left to right. Gunnery Sergeant Elia Fontecchio, called Gunny by the men of Kilo Company, saw it fly fifteen feet above the Humvee in front of him before detonating in the compounds or fields to its right. The Marines stopped the vehicles and dismounted the way they had rehearsed leaving camp that morning, this time watching front and back, left and right. Lance Corporal Hampton quickly searched the same garage that Major Carbins in the convoy had searched a short time earlier, and he found the same Iraqi mechanics huddled in the fetal position outside. He asked in gestures and broken Arabic where the firing had come from. One Iraqi shrugged. Another pointed south into the H-K Triangle.

Sergeant Stephen Reynolds, a sniper from Baltimore, noticed a white sports utility vehicle up ahead hurtling across Jade and into the farmlands north of town, obviously trying to skirt Marine checkpoints. A donkey cart lurched out of the SUV's way to avoid getting run down. Reynolds, who had tagged along with Dunham that morning to scope out vantage points at the police station, figured anyone that eager to avoid the Marines must be an insurgent. He told Captain Gibson about the SUV, but it was gone from view so quickly that they didn't pursue it.

The Marines took cover on the wedge of land between Diamond and Jade, and Captain Gibson found himself crouching next to Corporal Dunham. The captain told Dunham to send the gun trucks—the escort Humvees armed with machine guns and grenade launchers—around the neighborhood to block off the approaches south of the ambushers. The squad itself would move on foot through the H-K Triangle to hunt down whoever had fired the RPG at them. Corporal Dunham split the squad into two teams. The

Marines often divided patrols into satellite units that zig-zagged in almost random patterns toward their objectives. A team moving down one road might come to an intersection and spot other Marine teams on parallel streets, heading any which way. The idea was to confuse the enemy, but the Marines ran the risk of confusing themselves at the same time. The tactic required reliable radio communications to make sure that anyone who ran into trouble could get backup fast and to prevent Marines from accidentally shooting other Marines.

Captain Gibson set out with Lance Corporal Carbajal's eight-man team, fifty yards west of Dunham's team. They crossed Jade and hunkered down behind a wall and some small shops. Then they headed into the H-K Triangle, moving south, then west, then south again, then west again in a step pattern. Gummi Bear Covarrubias was the last man in the team, and he walked backward almost the entire way to fend off attacks from behind.

Corporal Dunham and Staff Sergeant Ferguson stuck with Lance Corporal Hampton's men. The two high-back Humvees stayed behind on Diamond. Normally, Lance Corporal Castaneda, known in the squad as Casta, was one of Dunham's point men, and he would walk well out ahead of the rest of the patrol poking through discarded bags and kicking cans to make sure that if a hidden bomb went off, it hit him and not his friends. But Lance Corporal Dean, who was driving one of the Humvees, didn't think it was a good idea to leave the two vehicles and their drivers without security, so he asked his buddy Casta to stay behind for protection. Casta was torn. He wanted to go out hunting with the squad, but he didn't want to leave Dean vulnerable to a surprise attack from the rear. Corporal Dunham ordered Casta to stick with Dean and the Humvees. As Dean headed back to the driver's seat, he turned to his friend Dunham. "Be careful, and kill one for me."

Dunham flashed his smile: "Oh, I will."

Gunny Fontecchio told Dean and the other Humvee driver, Lance Corporal Edwin Sopon, to park their vehicles behind a wall alongside Diamond. A twenty-nine-year-old blond weight lifter from Milford, Massachusetts, Gunny Fontecchio's job was to make sure the grunts had enough ammunition, food, and water, even if he had to ferry supplies between units in the middle of a firefight. The gunny also was in charge of making sure wounded men got evacuated to medical care. He tagged along with Dunham's men until he realized that they would be heading deep into the H-K Triangle. Then, worried about having left Dean, Casta, and Sopon isolated with the high-backs, he sprinted alone back to Diamond. Fontecchio figured the squad would eventually swing west toward Husaybah, so he and the high-back crews continued along Diamond toward the Husaybah arches. He couldn't raise the patrol's gun-truck escorts on the radio, and his transmissions to the Kilo fire teams kept breaking up as well. For the next ten minutes or so, Gunny Fontecchio, Dean, Casta, and Sopon had no idea where Dunham and his men were.

With Casta on guard duty with the high-back Humvees, Pfc. Miller stepped up to become Corporal Dunham's point man, a responsibility that weighed heavily on Kelly. He might be the first to get hit in an ambush. Or an insurgent might let him pass and detonate a roadside bomb to kill the men behind him. Either way, it was the point man's job to spot the enemy before the enemy spotted the patrol, and he was nervous that he might make a costly mistake. The first few blocks were quiet, as Miller led Dunham's seven-man team down an unpaved road that ran due south from the traffic circle. Each short block was made up of two or three dusty lots surrounded by yellow-tan stone walls and containing half-finished cinder-block homes. Miller steered the patrol one block to the west, then moved south again along a wide, uneven alleyway strewn with heavy chunks of concrete rubble, plastic shopping bags, and a few scrubby green weeds that clung stubbornly to the parched dirt. The patrol crossed one road where a large bus had stalled about fifty yards away pointing east; some Iraqi men were trying to get it moving again.

At about 12:20 p.m., the Marines reached the next cross street, where the alleyway hit a T-junction. On the left before the junction was an unfinished single-story home made of tan stone and poured concrete, with red metal doors and window grates. On the right, the alleyway widened out into the courtyard of a concrete-and-cinder-block house, a rusty, twisted car chassis lying forlornly amid the trash. Straight ahead, over some buildings and about a block away, they could see the top of a water treatment plant. The dirt lane that crossed in front of them was deeply rutted and, to their right, was bordered on the north side by a tumbledown stone wall and, a couple of dozen yards farther west, a head-height cinder-block wall. Stopped in the lane were eight vehicles, pointing east toward the approaching Marines. From the corner Dunham and his men could see a small bus, a van, a white Toyota Land Cruiser, a second SUV, a red tractor, a black BMW, a white truck frozen in the middle of an attempt to turn around in the narrow lane, and finally a white sedan with all four doors open.

The point man, Miller, had just reached the T-junction when Staff Sergeant Ferguson, a few dozen yards back, noticed the lineup of stopped vehicles. "What's going on?" he asked Corporal Dunham. "What are you doing?" Dunham wanted to keep moving, but Ferguson recalled the white SUV that Sergeant Reynolds had seen hightailing across Jade a few minutes earlier and thought the cars were worth a quick look. "No," Ferguson told Dunham. "We're going to search these cars."

Hampton walked alongside the small bus and peered through the windows. He saw only women and children and decided not to bother searching the interior. The driver of the second vehicle, the van, was middle-aged, with a younger man next to him. "Search vehicle," Hampton said in Arabic, a phrase he had picked up from the Marines' pocket language cards. He saw no weapons in the driver's lap, so he opened the sliding door on the van's right side. The cargo space contained nothing suspect.

Corporal Dunham and Pfc. Miller moved quickly up the street until they came to the elderly white Land Cruiser, which was some fifty yards from the intersection where the alleyway met the road. Miller edged along the passenger side and saw the muzzle and wood front grip of an AK-47 rifle poking out from under the floor mat. He looked up in time to see the driver, a young Iraqi man in a black tracksuit, open the door and lunge at Dunham.

The Iraqi wrapped his left arm around the back of Dunham's neck and cocked his right arm to punch the corporal in the face. Dunham caught the man's fist to block the swing.

The two stumbled toward the Land Cruiser. Dunham pulled his right knee up and drove it into the Iraqi's stomach. The Iraqi doubled over from the blow, and the men fell to the ground in an angry embrace.

Miller's brother, a sheriff's deputy in California, had bought Kelly a telescoping police baton and shipped it to Iraq. Miller didn't really think he'd ever need it, but he liked the idea of having one and kept it in a holster zip-tied to his flak vest. Up until that point, Miller had used it mostly to fend off stray dogs. But as he ran around the front of the SUV toward Dunham and the Iraqi, he pulled the baton out and snapped it down to his side to extend it to its full length. Miller saw the Iraqi lying on his back, his head toward the rear of the Land Cruiser. Dunham was face down on top of him, his torso rotated slightly counterclockwise.

Miller planted his left knee in the Iraqi's ribs. Bracing his left hand on Dunham's back, he slammed the butt of the baton as hard as he could into the Iraqi's forehead. The blow was so sharp that the metal baton collapsed back into itself. Miller was amazed that the man was still conscious, much less still fighting. He drove the baton into the Iraqi's forehead again, then jabbed it into the left side of the man's neck, a blood choke he had been told would pinch off circulation to the brain through the carotid artery.

Lance Corporal Hampton saw the melee and charged around the van and up the street, his adrenalin surging. All he could hear was the loud pounding of his own pulse as he searched for an open spot on the Iraqi to hit. *Shoot him in the head,* he said to himself. He aimed his rifle, but worried that any shot might go through the Iraqi and hit Miller. *Hell,* he thought, *I'll muzzle-thump him.* Marines are taught to poke their rifle barrels into the eyes of their enemies to make sure they're dead. Only the dead or comatose could resist flinching when poked hard in the eye with a long piece of metal. The muzzle-thump could also be delivered to the chest to get someone aggressive to back off without resorting to deadly force. Hampton planned to thump the Iraqi in the temple. If it knocked the man out, fine. If it killed him, that was fine with Bill, too. Hampton picked out a spot on the wriggling Iraqi's temple and pulled his rifle back to get some force behind it.

Lance Corporal Sanders, the radio operator, saw everything in slow motion: the Iraqi on his back, Dunham straddling him, Miller kneeling down and bashing the Iraqi's head with the baton, Hampton crossing the road and leaning in to help. Sanders, a bespectacled twenty-one-year-old with a tuft of curly blond hair and the soft twang of his native Oklahoma, kept a collection of photos next to his cot. There was a still life of his old blue pickup truck and another of his new blue pickup truck. There was a shot of him in tan coveralls and a green shirt, holding a Bud next to his stepfather, who held a can of his own in a foam holder. And there was a portrait in profile of his pregnant wife, Becca. The two met after high school and dated just two weeks before they got engaged. Sanders proposed over a spaghetti-and-meatball dinner a few weeks before the battalion shipped out to Kuwait for the invasion. Becca got pregnant while he was home between tours, and the day before the patrol to Karabilah she had told Sanders by satellite phone that the baby was a boy. Corporal Dunham had been one of the first people Sanders had shared the news with.

While Dunham, Miller, and Hampton wrestled with the Iraqi, Sergeant Reynolds, the sniper, told Sanders to provide cover in case the Iraqi had friends around. So Sanders was

more than a dozen yards away from the fight when he heard
Dunham yell a warning: "No, no, no—watch his hand!"
Hampton heard nothing except the beating of his own heart.
But he caught a fleeting glimpse of Dunham's helmet on the
ground next to the Iraqi. Dunham was on his stomach with
his arms stretched out in front of him and wrapped around
the sides of the helmet, as if he were holding it down on top
of something.

Then came the explosion.

The explosive was a British-made Mills Bomb, a classic
pineapple-shaped hand grenade. The user pulls a safety ring
pin out and squeezes the external lever—the spoon—until
he's ready to throw it. Then he releases the spoon, which falls
away, leaving the bomb armed. Typically, three to five seconds elapse between the time the spoon flies off and the
grenade explodes. Marines were taught to "milk" a grenade,
counting one, one-thousand, two, one-thousand, before
throwing it if the enemy was nearby. As they fought their
way into Baghdad in April 2003, a Marine from Third Battalion forgot to do so in one case, and the Iraqi fighter had
time to throw the grenade back at the Marines before it
blew up.

Bill Hampton saw a flash of light, but the explosion didn't
sound very loud to him. His vision blurred, and he knew that
something had happened to him. He just didn't know what.
His first thought was whether his teeth had been hit. He ran
his tongue along them and was relieved to find them all in
place. But his face, leg, and arm leaked red. The concussion
had broken his nose. One tiny metal fragment hit him under

the nostrils, and another embedded itself in his top lip. A piece of shrapnel about the size of a pen tip hit him in the right knuckle. Several shards of metal hit him in the left arm and left leg. One piece hit a bone in his forearm, broke up and opened an inch-wide hole as it exited. Another traveled up his arm and cut its way out of the inside of his elbow, leaving an X-shaped tear, then lodged in his biceps. He remembered that slowing his breathing would slow his bleeding and tried to do so. He staggered against the cinder-block wall and back toward the intersection. He couldn't lift his rifle with his left arm, so he held it in his right hand by the trigger guard and pistol grip, trying to keep an eye out for enemy fighters.

Kelly Miller saw the explosion and its aftermath in a series of still frames. First he saw Dunham tipping over, his radio headset still on but his helmet gone. Then Miller saw the sky as he fell over backward onto the rocket launcher slung from his shoulder. He heard a steady ring, like the sound a hospital heart monitor makes when the patient flatlines. Miller's face hurt and felt hot as if he had a bad sunburn. He tasted blood in his mouth and had the vague feeling that he was being shot at. His left arm hurt next. He tried to grab his rifle with his left hand, but nothing happened. He wondered why his arm wasn't working and looked down to see blood streaming off his fingertips.

One piece of hot metal had hit Miller's upper lip, traveled inside his right cheek and shattered a molar before coming to rest inside the back of his cheek. Other fragments peppered the area around his eyes, left cheek, and forehead. The blast blew out his left eardrum. One piece of grenade shrapnel went clean through his right triceps side-to-side and punctured the brachial artery, but for some reason it didn't hurt as badly as his upper left arm, which had been hit by five or six big chunks of metal and sprayed with pebble-sized fragments.

Miller stood up and grasped his rifle in his right hand. He briefly kneeled by the van in front of the Land Cruiser and complained to Staff Sergeant Ferguson about having bloodied his clean uniform. The blast had pushed Ferguson back, and the thud in his chest cavity reminded him of standing near the starting line when dragsters gunned their engines. Miller assured Ferguson that he was O.K., but added, "My mom is going to be fucking pissed."

Staff Sergeant Brad Baiotto brought up the rear in Corporal Dunham's team. He had come along that day to sign off on the payment to the Iraqi contractor who had done the repairs to the police station, but the contractor hadn't shown up. As Dunham headed south on the alleyway, Baiotto stopped before the T-junction to keep an eye on the stalled bus on the road north of the Marines. When the grenade exploded around the corner, it echoed so loudly that he thought it was a car bomb. Sergeant Reynolds, the sniper, thought the Iraqi must have been wired with explosives like a Palestinian suicide bomber. When he heard the blast, he crouched, looked up, and saw a cloud of smoke, dirt, and pieces of something that looked like fabric drifting above the street.

The explosion left Sanders, the radio operator, temporarily deaf. He saw Dunham, Miller, and Hampton knocked back by the blast and thought, *They're all fucking dead.* Sanders worked his way forward, aiming his rifle at the Iraqi man on the tractor farther back in line, a guy in the black sedan, and a couple of others. He was stunned to see Miller and Hampton get to their feet and stagger toward him along the cinder-block wall, their arms hung limp at their sides, glazed looks on their faces, blood sprayed on their tan cammies. "Get the fuck behind the wall!" Sanders yelled at them.

Sanders was still thirty feet away from the spot where the grenade had gone off when the Iraqi, who was flat on his back, sat up and faced him like a man startled in bed. Sanders could make out a dark red patch on the front of his tracksuit. The Iraqi rolled to his left, looking back at Sanders, his eyebrows raised in fear. He tried to stand and run, but skidded in place for an instant as his loafers lost traction on the dirt road. Finally he got to his feet and sprinted away without turning, blood dripping from his right arm. Sanders hesitated briefly at the shock of seeing a dead man rise, and the Iraqi made it two or three strides down the road before Sanders lifted his rifle and opened fire. The shots cut the Iraqi's legs out from under him, and he slammed face first into the dirt. His legs useless, the man tried to crawl away, grabbing at the dirt with his arms. Sanders killed him with another long burst. Later Sanders counted the rounds remaining in his magazine. There were five left; he had fired twenty-five shots at the Iraqi.

Reynolds thought there must have been a second Iraqi fighter somewhere nearby, since it seemed too hard to accept that the Iraqi wrestling with Dunham could have survived the blast. "Where's the other Iraqi?" he asked anyone and everyone. "Where's the guy who exploded?"

Sanders saw Dunham face down in the dirt ahead. "Cover me," he said to Staff Sergeant Ferguson. "I'm going there to get Dunham." Sanders ran up and took hold of the woven canvas handle on the back of Dunham's flak vest.

At the same moment, Staff Sergeant Baiotto came around the corner from the alleyway behind Ferguson, who was on the left side of the line of vehicles, watching for Iraqi gunmen farther down the lane. "Help me get my Marine out of here," Ferguson said to Baiotto. Baiotto ran forward and grasped Dunham's vest with both hands. Jason's head, covered in bright red, flopped loosely onto Baiotto's wrists and forearms. As the Marines lifted, Dunham's rifle fired once into the ground. Jason's hand had apparently brushed the trigger.

Bending down, Sanders and Baiotto dragged Dunham backward, his boot heels scraping along the dirt road, until an Iraqi gunman popped around a corner down the lane and fired a burst of six or eight rounds at them. The Marines put Dunham down and took cover behind one of the Iraqi vehicles. Ferguson fired four or five rounds in the Iraqi's general direction, ill-aimed shots intended to get the man to stop shooting. The Iraqi ducked around the corner, but Ferguson waited, his rifle raised and pointed at the spot where the man had disappeared. The Iraqi popped back into view an instant later, and Ferguson clearly saw his pale yellow shirt and black pants before the staff sergeant fired two quick shots at him. The man slipped back around the corner. Taking advantage of Ferguson's covering fire, Sanders and Baiotto pulled Dunham back toward the opening at the end of the cinder-block wall.

"It's Sanders, buddy, relax," Sanders told Dunham. "I'm gettin' you out."

Sergeant Reynolds saw Miller and Hampton wandering away from the explosion in a daze and grabbed them both by their bloody blouses. He sat them up against the north side of the wall, out of sight from the street. Miller wiped the smeared blood off his face with his sleeve, exposing the perforations below. Kelly saw raw muscle through a hole in his left arm and thought it was bone. "Aw fuck, my arm is broken," he moaned. "Fuck, fuck, fuck, fuck, fuck. Get me outta here, and get me morphine."

Hampton remained calm and told Reynolds to help Miller first. The sergeant wrapped Miller's left arm. Hampton leaned over to help and tried to keep Miller steady. "Breathe with me," Hampton said. When Miller's left arm was bandaged, Hampton and Reynolds saw the blood seeping through Miller's right sleeve from the punctured artery. Miller's head drooped forward.

Hampton's own sleeve was red, as well, and he sat forward to allow Reynolds to take his vest and other gear off. Hampton undid the top button on his own shirt, then Sergeant Reynolds ripped the rest of the buttons open and slipped the shirt off Hampton's shoulders to expose the shrapnel wounds. The sergeant took Hampton's first-aid kit off of his gear but struggled to open the vacuum-packed field dressings. "I'm glad you guys aren't bleeding to death," he joked. Reynolds bandaged Hampton's forearm. Hampton cut open his own pants from the knee down and wrapped his tattered leg in gauze.

As he sat waiting to be evacuated, Bill Hampton's thoughts turned to more mundane matters. He took off his watch and put it in his pocket, worried that the docs might cut the band if his arm swelled too much. He wanted to make absolutely sure that his privates were intact. So he propped himself up on his right knee, leaned his head against the cinder blocks, and peed as best he could, shortly before Miller edged toward the very same spot.

"Hey, you know he just pissed there," Reynolds warned Miller.

"I don't care," Miller said. "I need some drugs."

Miller turned to Hampton: "Don't lie to me," he said. "Is my face fucked up?"

"Look at my face," Hampton replied. "What do you think?" Miller lay down, using his flak vest as a pillow.

After he and Baiotto pulled Dunham to the street side of the cinder-block wall, Sanders radioed for a helicopter to take out the wounded. "Medevac, medevac," he said. "One urgent."

First Lieutenant Chris McManus had been camped out in the desert for the last three days, waiting for something to happen. Lieutenant Colonel Lopez thought it prudent to have a few gun trucks not too far away, ready to help any Marines who got into a tight spot. So McManus and his men were waiting with four Humvees six miles from the H-K Triangle when he heard the radio call. "This is Sanders. We got three casualties."

The lieutenant was shocked not so much by the report of casualties, but that the radio actually worked at such a long range. "We're en route," McManus responded. He thought Sanders sounded nervous.

"We've got one that's pretty bad," Sanders said.

Lieutenant McManus and the gun trucks drove to Market Street and turned south on East End. When they reached Train they picked up Doc Chops, Hospitalman Third Class Lynott, who was with the Lima Company Marines searching houses after the firefight at the Crackhouse. The doc had heard a radio summons for "any corpsman" and jumped into one of the passing gun trucks. McManus's Humvee then turned left into the H-K Triangle and drove under a train trestle. In his hurry, the driver didn't notice the approaching five-foot drop, and the Humvee slammed nose first into the ground below before bouncing back up. The impact launched the standing turret gunner past his machine gun and antitank missile launcher and over the roof until he found himself dangling upside down in front of the windshield, looking back in at the driver. He scrambled back into the turret, and the Humvees sped around the water treatment plant near the train tracks and up to the road where Dunham had been hit.

Doc Chops saw Corporal Dunham lying next to the cinder-block wall, his blood oozing into the dirt in a macabre halo. His eyes were swollen shut, and the skin on his forehead was folded crudely back. The doc searched Dunham's body for other injuries but found only a small nick on his neck. The corpsman didn't have a support collar, so he tried to stabilize Dunham's head by strapping a brown plastic "Meal, Ready-to-Eat" bag to each side. Dunham pushed the MREs away. Doc Chops wrapped the corporal's head and eyes in white gauze. Dunham waved his arm and tried to remove the gauze. He made gurgling noises, but said nothing. Doc Chops inserted an IV drip to keep him hydrated. Once he had stabilized Dunham, the corpsman walked around the wall to check on Miller and Hampton. They asked whether Jason was all right. "To be honest with you, I really don't know," Doc Chops responded.

"I hope they got that son of a bitch," Miller said. During the confusion, one of the Marines found himself a helmet short and asked Miller for his. Miller first removed the photo he kept inside of his mother Linda and girlfriend Shannon. The helmet ended up with Doc Chops, who wore Miller's bloodstains for months.

When the situation on the street quieted, Sanders came around the wall to check on Miller and Hampton. "Did you get the guy?" Hampton asked him.

"Yeah, I got the guy," Sanders said. But, he added, "Dunham's not good."

Gunny Fontecchio had picked up Sanders's medevac call while he, Dean, Sopon, and Castaneda were driving around the city trying to find Kilo Four-Two. When he arrived with the two high-back Humvees, the gunny saw Dunham's motionless body. He leaped out of the passenger seat, climbed into the open Humvee bed, and tossed out MRE crates and boxes of plastic water bottles. He yanked out the bench that ran down the center and threw it out onto the street, as well.

At first, Lance Corporal Mark Dean couldn't identify the Marine stretched out on the ground next to the cinder-block wall, with the top of his head bandaged, his camouflage blouse open, and an IV running into his right arm. The face, bloated and bloodied, didn't look familiar. Then he saw the tattoo on the man's chest—the ace of spades, the skull munching on the eight ball—and realized he was looking at one of his best friends. "Dunham, if you can hear me, give me a sign," Dean begged. Jason didn't speak, although Dean noticed his left leg move a bit. "You killed that bastard," Dean told him. "That bastard's dead." Dean prayed to himself and spoke aloud to Jason to try to keep him steady, a trick he had learned dealing with victims of car wrecks as a volunteer firefighter back in Oklahoma. "You're going to be all right," said Dean. "We're going to get you home."

The Marines loaded Dunham head first into the bed of Gunny Fontecchio's Humvee on top of a layer of Kevlar blankets. "I'm taking him to the helo," the gunny told Doc Chops.

"I'm driving," Dean announced, even though it wasn't his

Humvee. Casta jumped in next to him and poked his rifle out the window. He scanned the crowds for insurgents and shouted encouragement to Dunham as they flew up Route Jade and Market Street, two gun trucks racing along as escorts. In back, Gunny Fontecchio squatted by Jason and held his bandaged head off the floor as they drove two miles to Lima Company's base, Camp Husaybah. Fontecchio watched Jason's chest rise and fall in shallow breaths and worried that he might choke on his own blood or tongue. He saw clear fluid dripping out of both of Jason's ears, mixed with blood.

"You're going to be all right. You're not going to die," Fontecchio told Jason. "We're going to get you out of here real soon. We're on our way to the helo. You're doing really great. Keep breathing, keep breathing." Jason showed no sign that he had heard. *God, I hope he makes it,* Fontecchio said to himself.

Hospitalman Second Class Danny White, a reservist who installed pacemakers in cardiac patients in civilian life, was at Camp Husaybah when he saw the Humvee pull in. He hopped aboard and directed Dean to LZ Parrot. As they drove, he turned Jason's head to make sure his airway was clear and heard a gurgling sound as if his trachea were partly blocked. He reached inside Jason's mouth and moved his tongue to the side. He briefly considered trying a trick he'd heard that medics used in the Vietnam War—safety-pinning Jason's tongue to his lower lip to make sure he didn't swallow it. But the doc noticed Jason breathing more smoothly and decided it wasn't necessary.

At the landing zone, Doc White slipped a brace around Dunham's neck as they loaded him onto a stretcher and a Blackhawk air ambulance touched down in the parking lot. Doc White believed the corporal's wounds were so severe that he wouldn't live, and he guessed the medical officer would decide that Dunham should wait at the LZ until Marines with survivable wounds had been flown to the battalion shock-trauma unit in al Qa'im. It wasn't Doc White's call, but he mentioned the possibility aloud and found Lance Corporal Dean looking at him in murderous fury. Dean watched the medevac proceedings with growing frustration. He felt the rescue was taking far too long and kept thinking about the civilian emergency squad's guiding motto, Life over Limb, which meant that medics should concentrate on making sure the victim survived and put off treating less severe wounds until later. "I'm a paramedic—I know what I'm doing," Dean said angrily. "That's my buddy up there, and these docs need to get up there now." Dean harangued the docs until a first sergeant ordered him to back off and let the corpsmen do their jobs in peace.

Doc White was relieved when a second Blackhawk landed and he realized there would be room enough for all the wounded men. Gunny Fontecchio's legs had fallen asleep squatting in the Humvee, and he found he couldn't stand well enough to help carry Dunham's litter to the helicopter. The Blackhawk rose up, tilted its nose downward, and sped Dunham toward al Qa'im.

Pfc. Miller and Lance Corporal Hampton arrived at LZ Parrot a few minutes later, sitting on the floor of a high-back Humvee bed. Hampton held his rifle in his good arm, aiming out the back. Miller had thrown up before getting into the Humvee at the scene of the grenade attack, and every bump on the way to the landing zone sent shooting pain through his arms. Gunny Fontecchio met their Humvee and told Hampton that Dunham had been breathing on his own when he got on the helo. "I want to stay," Hampton told the gunny, but both men knew he was in no shape for more combat.

Miller was on his feet, if a bit unsteady. "I'm pissed off, Gunny," Miller told Fontecchio, his face speckled with blood and one arm in a sling. "I just wanna kill the fuckers." Then he vomited.

Back in Oklahoma, Lance Corporal Dean used to chase tornadoes for thrills and sell video footage to the local news station. In Iraq, Dean documented his war with a video camera he stashed in his gear. He liked to put it on the dashboard of the Humvee during patrols or shoot a few frames when roadside bombs blew up. Sometimes he'd aim the camera at himself and narrate a scene for his wife Becky Jo. The video collection he kept in the barracks at al Qa'im was a collage of his life in the Marines: Dunham and a few Marine friends shooting Dean's .45 pistol at a blue cigarette lighter perched on some scrap metal near Twentynine Palms. The platoon at a desert camp in Kuwait, playing cards in a big Bedouin tent. A smiling Dunham, his head shaved, happily raising his middle finger to the camera. Lance Corporal Hampton, Corporal Dunham, and others playing Frisbee in camp, and then carefully holding up strands of sharp razor wire while Pfc. Miller, the boot, slithered underneath to retrieve a stray throw. The platoon flying from Kuwait into Iraq, joking about how many Marines were on board and how few parachutes. Dean instructing the others in the plane to chant: "We're going to Iraq, and we're coming back." Dunham, in sunglasses, walking toward the huge gray transport helicopter that would take him to al Qa'im, turning to the camera with a big dimpled

grin on his face and sticking his tongue out. Dunham smok-
ing a water pipe and blowing smoke rings with Jordanian
special operations troops. The squad sleeping in full combat
gear in Husaybah while mortars rained down outside.

At LZ Parrot, Dean placed his video camera on the
Humvee and filmed Kelly Miller walking to the medevac
helo and collapsing like a flat tire onto the stretcher.

————————

Plagued by bad radio communications, Lance Corporal Carbajal's fire team had been largely unaware of the fighting in
the H-K Triangle, even though they were just a few blocks
away when the grenade exploded. After Corporal Dunham
had split the patrol into two teams on Route Diamond, Carbajal's men moved south on a path roughly parallel to Dunham's, but farther to the west, searching cars and houses as
they went. In one compound the Marines found three Iraqis.
Two obeyed immediately when the Marines ordered them
to come out. The third Iraqi, a man, remained still. The
Marines yelled at him, but it turned out he was deaf. Lance
Corporal Polston, one of the boots, was amazed how close
they had come to shooting a deaf man for failing to listen.

On the way, Carbajal's team split again into two smaller
groups that lost track of each other. Captain Gibson, a corpsman, and Sam, the company's Kurdish translator, ended up in
a dry wadi and open lot between Husaybah and the H-K
Triangle. As the captain relieved himself on a rock pile, he
heard a few bursts of gunfire from the southeast, but didn't
know it was Dunham's men. He turned and saw civilian cars
backing up along the narrow streets, trying to escape the
fighting. One Iraqi man carrying a black bag hopped into a

waiting car, and the captain yelled at the corpsman: "Stop those fucking vehicles." Gibson, the corpsman, and Sam blocked the cars, and the Iraqis inside explained that they were headed to a wedding. Sam, who carried his own pistol, opened the trunk and found it full of wedding gifts. The black bag contained a colorful wedding dress.

Carbajal and Gibson eventually found each other, and moved south toward the train tracks that skirted Husaybah and Karabilah. They set up a checkpoint to stop cars driving along the rail lines, and saw Lieutenant McManus's gun trucks fly by, but didn't know they were on their way to deliver Doc Chops to help Dunham. Carbajal's team was no more than four hundred yards from Dunham's team, separated by the walled water treatment plant and a few houses. But the radios still didn't work, and the captain remained unaware that there had been any casualties. Eventually Carbajal broke into the water treatment plant and climbed a staircase onto the roof. He looked north and saw Staff Sergeant Ferguson on the narrow street where Dunham had lain just a few minutes earlier. "What's going on?" he shouted down to Ferguson.

"We have three WIAs," Ferguson yelled back, using the military shorthand for wounded in action.

"Who?" Carbajal asked.

Bill Hampton was Carbajal's best friend, and Carbajal was furious. He guided Captain Gibson to the narrow lane and the remaining members of Dunham's team. Ferguson reported that Miller and Hampton were O.K. The way he said it made the captain suspect that someone else wasn't O.K. "What do you mean?" Gibson asked. Ferguson told him Dunham was badly wounded. The captain felt a wave of guilt wash over him. He hadn't been there for the fight. He hadn't even known his men had been hurt.

After the medevac helos took off, Lance Corporal Dean drove back to the scene of the attack and filmed the dead Iraqi lying on his stomach where Sanders had shot him, his eyes closed and head turned to the right. The Iraqi looked to be in his late twenties, with a clean-shaven face and prominent nose. His left arm was raised as if flagging a taxi, his right arm tight by his side. The man's thick, curled black hair was lifted into a visor where one of Sanders's shots, which had entered the back of his head, had broken through his forehead, pushing out the skull and a lump of white brain. The jacket of his tracksuit had a maroon stripe down each sleeve and was hiked up on his left side, revealing a white undershirt below. His black loafers were pointed awkwardly to the left, as if his feet were no longer connected to the bullet-riddled legs above.

The Marines removed a small arsenal from the man's Land Cruiser and propped the weapons up against the stone wall on the south side of the street. There was a pair of RPG launchers with spare grenades. There were two AK-47 rifles, the cheap, reliable weapon of Middle Eastern despots, African child soldiers, and South American revolutionaries alike, instantly recognizable by its banana-shaped magazine. A second Mills Bomb hand grenade was in front of the driver's seat of the Toyota. The Marines also found a loose grenade pin on the floor, which they figured came from the Mills Bomb that had wounded Dunham. The Iraqi, they thought, must have had the grenade armed and ready when he rushed out of the car, either in his hand or tucked in a belt or pocket even as he tried to throttle the corporal.

Gibson ordered the Marines to search every house in the neighborhood for hidden insurgents. As he gave his orders, the captain called Lance Corporal Carbajal "Kilo Four-Deuce," a sign that Dunham's squad was now his. Carbajal, who had clashed with Corporal Dunham over how tough to be with the boots, found the call sign disconcerting. He wanted to make squad leader; he didn't want it to happen like this. Sam the translator pointed his pistol at the locals sideways, like a street-gang member in a movie, as the Marines rummaged through the homes. Sanders was exhausted and desperately wanted the day to end. He was sick of the fighting, the war, the whole thing. He knelt listlessly on the street guarding the backs of the Marines inside the houses. The Marines detained four Iraqis, covering their heads with empty sandbags.

Captain Gibson paced the street where Dunham, Miller, and Hampton had been hit and noticed a piece of shredded olive-drab fabric on the ground. At first he thought it was part of a Humvee door or tarpaulin. Then by a stone wall he spotted another piece, larger, that clearly had once been the left half of a Kevlar helmet. By the cinder-block wall across the lane he found the right half. Gibson asked the men if they had seen Dunham's helmet. The Marines looked around their feet and realized they were surrounded by tiny bits of Kevlar, its once-hard form expanded into a loose fabric. Captain Gibson was stumped by what he saw. The only explanation he could think of was that the grenade had exploded in Dunham's face and blown his helmet to pieces.

The Marines picked up the Kevlar scraps and stuffed them into the cargo pockets of their fatigue pants and the pouches where they carried their night-vision goggles. Captain Gibson hated the idea of leaving Marine gear on the street, evidence of vulnerability for the enemy to see. Months later, when three Kilo Company Marines were torn apart by a rocket that struck the bed of a high-back Humvee, it drove Gibson to distraction that he couldn't confirm that the men's severed arms had been recovered.

Around 5 p.m., the captain came up with the idea of putting a watch on the dead Iraqi's body to see if anyone would come to claim it. Gibson couldn't find a building with a good enough view of the Iraqi where he lay, so he decided to move the body. Sanders looked at the man's brains bulging out of his head and thought, *Fucking idiot.* He kicked dirt onto the stain in the street left by Dunham's wound, disturbed to see American blood on foreign soil. He and Carbajal each lifted one of the Iraqi's legs; Captain Gibson and Castaneda hoisted the dead man by his armpits. Carbajal had never held a dead body before, and he clutched the man's pant leg to avoid touching the body itself. The man was already stiff. His brains slipped out of his skull, and his loafers fell off in the move. The Marines left the body face up in a wide compound so anyone who knew the man would recognize him.

Captain Gibson carried a stack of business cards with him. The original idea was to give them to the Iraqi contacts, contractors, and friends the Marines hoped to meet. But as hostilities intensified, they became death cards instead, left to let the insurgents know exactly whom they were up against. Gibson placed his card on the Iraqi's body. It had the red-and-blue logo of the First Marine Division, its World War II service commemorated by the word "Guadalcanal" written down the middle. There was the chiseled arrowhead, horse, and bayonet logo of Kilo Company, and the gold eagle, globe, and anchor of the Marine Corps. In English on one side and Arabic on the other it read:

Kilo Company
3rd Battalion, 7th Marines
United States Marine Corps
Captain Trent A. Gibson
Commanding Officer
K 3/7

At the bottom was the motto of the First Marine Division: *"No Better Friend, No Worse Enemy."*

Gibson, Sanders, and Reynolds, the sniper, climbed to the second story of a building with a clear shot at the body, and waited for an hour. Sanders put a pinch of Copenhagen snuff inside his lower lip. Carbajal and the others took turns watching from the rooftop and staircase window at the water treatment plant. Staff Sergeant Ferguson stared at the Iraqi's body and thought back to the conversation at Camp Husaybah a few weeks earlier, and to Dunham's stubborn conviction that a helmet would blunt the blast of a grenade. He suddenly knew what Jason had done.

When nobody showed up to claim the dead Iraqi, Captain Gibson decided to extend the vigil all night and bring in a team of snipers. During the shift change, however, someone made off with the body unseen.

The remnants of Corporal Dunham's patrol rolled into the base at al Qa'im as the sky darkened into evening. The four Iraqi prisoners were cuffed and hooded in the back of a high-back Humvee. The Marines parked near the shower trailers and tossed the prisoners out onto the paved parking lot. The Iraqis landed blind and hard, some on their shoulders, one on his head. The grunts punched and kicked the prisoners until they grew worried that an officer would see them from the nearby battalion command post. They frog-marched the Iraqis toward the camp detention facility and stopped outside, pounding them some more until an alarmed staff sergeant rushed out of the prison and stopped the beatings. The staff sergeant asked what had happened. One of the Marines told him about Dunham and then burst into tears.

When other Marines saw Lance Corporal Sanders arrive back at the base they congratulated him for killing the Iraqi who had attacked Dunham. He didn't respond. He washed his face, stretched out on his cot, and stayed there for three days, speaking to no one. On April 17, when the town of Husaybah erupted in a daylong battle, he heard the gunfire and lay in bed thinking, *Do I want to go? Nobody's making me.* Then he put on his flak vest and helmet and jumped into a Humvee heading toward Husaybah.

VI | *Shock-Trauma Tent*

Al Qa'im, Iraq

EVEN IN A TIME of smart bombs and aerial drones, the Marines envisioned war as a frenzied bayonet charge into enemy lines. During the invasion of Iraq, Lieutenant Colonel Mike Belcher, Matt Lopez's predecessor as commander of Third Battalion, had ordered his Marines to fix their bayonets to the barrels of their rifles whenever they encountered the enemy, and to embrace the "intimate brutality" of the bayonet thrust. He believed the sight of fixed bayonets would bolster his men's esprit and frighten the daylights out of the Iraqi defenders. "We will instill fear in our enemies by mastering the art of bayonet fighting and fostering the physical and mental strength to engage in it," Belcher wrote in a three-page memo to his men outlining the battalion's "edged weapons policy." The knife imagery was everywhere around battalion headquarters in the rail yards of al Qa'im. The battalion's radio call sign was Blade, its emblem a downward-pointing bayonet, and its nickname "The Cutting Edge."

So the hand-painted plywood sign in front of the camp's house of worship that read "Cutting Edge Chapel" was a reference not to some heretical faith being practiced inside, but rather to the warrior mentality of the worshipers. The chapel was a makeshift affair in a stripped-down Iraqi railroad carriage parked on the tracks that ran through the middle of the base. Neatly arranged on the plywood floor were rows of red plastic patio chairs, which served as pews for the Marines who dropped in for services or postcombat group therapy sessions with Chaplain David Slater. Lieutenant Slater had joined the Navy three years earlier at the age of forty-three. A pastor in upstate New York at the time, he had been growing restless and fled to the woods for a spiritual retreat. When he emerged, he found a Navy recruiting letter in his mailbox, which he interpreted as a sign from above. After some hesitation, the Navy waived the usual age limits and let him in.

Lieutenant Slater was in his narrow sanctuary just after noon on April 14 when he heard the roar of a Blackhawk helicopter lifting off and speeding west toward Husaybah. He knew that sound was a sign that in fifteen or twenty minutes the birds would be back with fresh Marine casualties for the Navy shock-trauma platoon. He walked across the tracks to the trauma tent and prepared to soothe. What he found was chaos, as nine wounded Marines—1 percent of the entire battalion—arrived within a period of fifteen minutes.

The Navy medical team in al Qa'im led a more informal lifestyle than the combat Marines they cared for. Everyone lived together in the same air-conditioned Bedouin tent, men and women, enlisted and officers, middle-aged doctors and twenty-something corpsmen. After a few months the older officers got fed up with the rap music, indoor skateboarding, and "post adolescent hormone driven behavior, which gives us a constant source of amusement and/or irritation," Commander Ed Hessel, a forty-four-year-old emergency physician, wrote to his family in Eugene, Oregon. The doctors finally managed to talk their way into more sedate housing in a nearby warehouse.

A calm, bespectacled man with a receding buzz cut and a variety of University of Oregon Ducks paraphernalia, Ed Hessel relished the small triumphs of camp life: finding cold milk in the morning for his Raisin Bran Crunch; the arrival of new porta-potties to replace the ones whose seats were so cracked that they pinched his rear when he sat down; the time a Marine broke the backboard during a pickup basketball game and used an Abrams tank as a ladder while he welded it back together. Dr. Hessel had an Internet connection and got the news from the BBC on shortwave. Considering he was in the middle of a desert war zone, not much was missing. Hessel jokingly ended one letter home: "P.S. Send liquor, porn, and pork."

Ed was awed by the young men who went running toward danger and disturbed to see so many of them coming back on bloody stretchers. But April 14 was far beyond anything he had seen so far. The first evac helicopter arrived at 12:30 p.m., carrying the wounded from the Crackhouse: Corporal Lightfoot with his gouged foot, Lance Corporal Roshak with the wedge of wood sticking out of his head, and the Iraqi civilian whose car had been machine-gunned by Marines. Lance Corporal Falah, the colonel's Kuwaiti-born bodyguard who had been shot in the convoy ambush, followed minutes later in the next bird.

Corporal Vilaire Lazard ran the seven-man Marine team that provided security and heavy lifting for the Navy trauma and surgical units. While the Blackhawk was in the air he had

gotten word that there was a wounded Iraqi on board, so he
met the helo when it landed on the pad next to the medical
tents. The Iraqi was a slender young man, with long sideburns and a pair of black Superman curls hanging down onto
his forehead. His chin showed a few days' growth of beard,
trimmed into a goatee, his left cheek was streaked with
blood, and his torso was perforated with bullet wounds. Corporal Lazard didn't know who the man was or how he had
been wounded, but to be safe he assumed the Iraqi was an
insurgent fighter and ordered his men to put the stretcher on
the ground outside the trauma tent. The corporal, a twenty-
two-year-old from Miami, then drew his pistol from his
shoulder holster and used his free hand to search the Iraqi for
arms and explosives. "Mister, water," the man begged.

After the initial frisk, Corporal Lazard told a corpsman to
cut off the man's remaining clothes to allow a more thorough
search. Then four Marines carried the Iraqi naked into the
trauma tent, while Corporal Lazard pointed his pistol at the
man's head. The corporal didn't have a round in the firing
chamber, but he suspected the sight of the weapon would be
enough to persuade the Iraqi to do as he was told, without
need for translation. He decided the man's head was the safest
target, since, in case he actually had to fire, he didn't want to
hit the Marines standing at the corners of the litter. The Iraqi
appeared frightened of the corporal and his pistol, shaking his
hands vigorously from side to side when their eyes made
contact.

The trauma tent was the first stop for incoming casualties,
and Dr. Hessel's team was charged with stabilizing the wounded
before sending them into surgery or on to the next hospital.
The tent's green floor and white walls gave off a rubbery
aroma, and an American flag hung from the ceiling. Clumps of

stethoscopes dangled like bananas from the ceiling, above olive drab trunks containing chest tubes, bandages, and emergency airway tubes.

Finally confident that the Iraqi was unarmed, Lazard and his men carried the stretcher into the tent and placed it on the metal sawhorses at the first of the three casualty stations. The corporal cuffed the man's ankles and wrists with plastic ties. As the doctors did their work, the corporal looked down at the Iraqi, and the Iraqi looked up at the corporal.

Having seen the Iraqi come in under guard, the medical staff entered him into their computer records as POW #1. Dr. Hessel rolled the naked man from his back to his side and found several gunshot wounds, including holes in his chest and a gaping exit wound on his back just under his right shoulder. Bullet entry wounds tend to be small punctures, but the projectiles tear away the flesh as they leave the body, much in the same way that a nail enters a board cleanly and then creates splinters as it punches through the other side. The doctor didn't want the man causing a ruckus, so he gave him morphine to quiet him down, then uncuffed his wrists. He left the ankles cuffed.

Hospitalman First Class John Padilla, a senior corpsman who assisted Dr. Hessel in the trauma tent, worried most about a sucking chest wound that had punctured the man's right lung. Every time the Iraqi inhaled, air leaked out of his lung into the surrounding chest cavity. When he exhaled, the air remained in his chest cavity, leaving less room for the lung itself to expand the next time. With every breath, there was more air in the chest cavity and less in the lung. Eventually, the man's lung would collapse, starving him of oxygen and putting pressure on his heart and good lung.

The chest tube that the corpsman at Camp Husaybah had

inserted through the Iraqi's entry wound should have helped relieve the pressure. The tube's one-way valve was designed to allow air to escape the chest cavity and block it from reentering through the bullet hole. The idea was to reduce the air pressure around the lung and allow the lung itself to fully inflate. Despite the chest tube, Doc Padilla could hear no sound of breathing from the wounded lung, and he noticed that the man was gasping with his good lung. Dr. Hessel inserted a second chest tube and sutured it off. Doc Padilla, a stocky thirty-four-year-old Texan, covered the wound with an airtight dressing made of Vaseline gauze, hooked up an intravenous line, and fed in antibiotics. The approach worked, and the Iraqi's breathing grew less labored.

In the next litter over lay Lance Corporal Falah, a red gash torn into his left biceps. Falah's wound had damaged the nerves in his arm and was agonizingly painful. But he reveled in what he had already decided was the proudest day of his life; he had taken a bullet for the United States, for the Marines, and for his colonel. The potent mix of pain, pride, and, finally, morphine left him animated if only moderately coherent. He yelled "Oorah" and "Semper fi" as the Marines escorted him off the helicopter. Once settled onto a stretcher in the trauma tent he loudly proclaimed, "I love America."

At first, Dr. Hessel looked askance at the loud Arab with the tourniquet around his upper arm and figured he was a captured Iraqi fighter trying to weasel his way out of trouble. *Yeah—now you love America,* he said to himself. Then he spotted Falah's camouflage fatigues and realized Falah was both a loud Arab and a loud Marine. "God loves me," Falah said to no one in particular. "America loves me." Falah was dismayed, however, when he realized that Lieutenant Colonel Lopez was still somewhere in Husaybah without him. "Where's the colonel?" he asked the doctors. "They left the colonel out there? I love the colonel." He vented his fury at the Iraqi prisoner on the next stretcher, shouting Arabic insults interspersed with English taunts of "You fucking dog" and "You fucking goat." For good measure he added, "I'm going to kill Osama bin Laden and piss on his body."

Though animated, Falah was in serious condition. The surgeons had to restore the blood flow to his lower arm within a few hours of the injury or he'd lose the limb. As the surgeons inserted anesthesia into his IV, Falah sang the Marine Corps Hymn through the oxygen mask. "From the Halls of Montezuma to the Shores of Tripoli," he began. He didn't get very far into the song before he lost consciousness. The surgeons, wearing shorts and T-shirts under their gowns to stay cool, found the loose upper end of the artery and put a clamp on it. Then they stretched the end of the blood vessel over a thin plastic tube, much as a radiator hose slips over a fitting in a car. They tied a length of braided white cotton umbilical tape around the overlapping section to hold the artery and tube together and seal the connection. In the same way, they connected the other end of the tube to the severed artery closer to Falah's elbow. When they released the clamp at the top of Falah's arm, the blood immediately flowed through the plastic tube and back into the arteries and veins below. The surgeons saw Falah's hand turn pink and felt the pulse return to his wrist.

When Falah woke up in the recovery tent, he resumed his discourse on the battalion commander. "You'd better take care of my colonel," he warned the surgeon, a sixty-year-old Navy captain. The doctors told him the colonel was fine, but Falah didn't believe them. At some point, Chaplain Slater appeared at Falah's side and assured him that Jesus loved him.

Falah burst into tears and said, "I love you, Jesus." Then he passed out.

At 12:45 p.m., as Falah was being ferried to the surgical tent, the next wave of wounded Marines began arriving from Husaybah. First among them was Corporal Dunham, who took Falah's spot in the center station of the trauma ward. When a wounded Marine was conscious, Chaplain Slater made small talk—asked his name, hometown and the like— to help keep the patient calm and alert even in the face of horrific wounds. The chaplain saw no sign, however, that Jason was aware of what was happening. Slater gently held Jason's hand for five minutes, then moved on to the patients he thought he could help.

The medical team snipped away at Jason's clothes until he lay naked except for the neck brace and head bandage. Dr. Hessel searched carefully through the blood and pulp on the side of Jason's head and guessed that he had been hit by three grenade fragments. One, he thought, had penetrated the left side of his skull not far behind his eye. The second had entered the brain slightly higher and farther toward the back of his head. The third had punctured his neck, but didn't go in very far. Jason's heart rate and blood pressure were stable, but he had begun "posturing"—an almost fetal curling of the arms and clenching of the fists that signaled serious injury to the brain.

Dr. Hessel concluded that Jason was "unarousable" and felt that whatever hope remained could not be tapped at a field hospital in the desert. Al Qa'im didn't have so much as an X-ray machine, much less more advanced diagnostic equipment. Hessel wanted Jason out on the next medevac flight to the surgical hospital at al Asad, and from there to the neurosurgical unit in Baghdad. In his heart, however, Ed was pessimistic. He just hoped to keep Jason alive long enough to get home to his family.

To increase Jason's chances of making it that far, Hessel wanted to relieve the corporal's brain and body of the effort required to breathe. And he wanted to make sure the corporal experienced no violent physical reactions that might add to the pressure on his already swollen brain. He had a nurse insert an intravenous drip and push in a series of drugs to sedate the corporal, paralyze his muscles, and blunt the gag response in his throat.

Lieutenant Bull Robinson, Corporal Dunham's platoon commander, was at the al Qa'im base when the wounded began arriving. One of the worst things about being injured in combat, Robinson thought, is that the wounded Marine is immediately separated from the people who can best comfort him—his buddies. Robinson knew some of the Lima Company Marines from his platoon's long stay at Camp Husaybah, and he wanted to make sure the wounded men at least saw a familiar face when they got off the Blackhawk. He rushed to the trauma tent and talked to Falah, Lightfoot, and the other casualties who had been aboard the first helicopters. The lieutenant then returned to the Kilo Company command post, only to learn that some of his own men had been hit as well, and he raced back and forth between the radio and the helipad trying to figure out who had been hurt and how badly. He missed Dunham's helicopter when it landed, but saw the next one arrive with Pfc. Kelly Miller and Lance Corporal Bill Hampton aboard. Miller had powder burns all over his face from the hand grenade blast and slipped in and out of consciousness while the trauma crew bandaged his shrapnel wounds. At one point Miller awoke and asked how Corporal Dunham was doing. Hampton insisted that the medical team treat Miller and the others before he would accept care himself. Then he limped off the helicopter and briefed the lieutenant on what had happened in the H-K Triangle.

Robinson walked to the rear door of the trauma tent and peeked in through the flap just in time to see the doctors feed a ventilator tube down the throat of a Marine with a bandaged head, muscular chest, and slim waist. The lieutenant knew immediately who it was. He feared the worst as he watched Doc Padilla press the plastic ventilator bag to force air into Jason's lungs. The lieutenant looked in a few more times until someone spotted him and zipped the door shut.

Corporal Matt Thompson from the sniper team was in the trauma station next to Dunham, his left thigh bone so badly shattered that the surgeon thought it looked as if an extra knee joint had been added to his leg. The hours that followed were a blur for Matt. He remembered hearing Falah above the din, proclaiming his love for the colonel. He remembered the painful sensation of an old man sticking a finger up his rectum to check for bleeding. He remembered wondering if he could keep his bloody fatigue pants as a souvenir. He remembered being strapped to a traction machine that pulled his leg straight and eased the pain. He remembered the pleasant rush of the morphine. He remembered only one phone number, his fiancée's, and borrowed a satellite phone to make a call. "Baby, I got shot," he told her.

In the afternoon, the doctors took Thompson to the operating tent. Thompson worried that the anesthetic wouldn't work and that he'd be awake for the operation. Instead, he went under immediately, and the surgeon used a device much like an old-style bit and brace to drill holes in his shin and upper thigh, on either side of the break. With no X-ray to guide him, the surgeon had to perform the procedure by feel. He then inserted stainless steel pins in the holes and connected them with a graphite frame that spanned Thompson's knee and held his leg together.

When the Blackhawk was ready, the trauma team wrapped Corporal Dunham in a jungle camouflage blanket and strapped him to the stretcher on top of the shredded remains of his fatigues. Doc Padilla rested the IV bag on Jason's belly for the short walk to the helicopter pad. "One and two and three and four—breathe," Padilla counted to himself as he walked hunched down next to the stretcher, squeezing the ventilator bag and squinting in the afternoon glare.

At 2:25 p.m., the Blackhawk took off for al Asad with Corporal Dunham, Lance Corporal Roshak, the wounded Iraqi civilian, now a prisoner, and Captain Lewis, the lawyer who had been shot three times during the convoy ambush. The sight of the giant splinter sticking out of Kevin Roshak's head had made even the seasoned denizens of the trauma platoon gasp, and a corpsman had asked Roshak to pose for a portrait. "This doesn't happen every day," the corpsman explained. The photo showed Kevin in profile, with his shirt off. The wedge of wood and nails protruded downward from under his left ear, levering the lobe outward. A spray of bright red radiated out from the entry point. On Kevin's face was the petrified look of a man crossing a frozen lake and hearing the crack of ice breaking beneath his feet. The doctors decided it would be safer to remove the splinter at the larger al Asad surgical hospital, in case the wood had pierced an artery.

Corporal Dunham lay directly above the Iraqi prisoner

aboard the Blackhawk. The nurse sat in a jump seat facing Jason and squeezed his ventilator bag twelve or fifteen times a minute. The Army pilots, told that a high-altitude flight might aggravate Jason's head injury, flew at 170 miles per hour less than fifty feet off the ground. They made the trip east to al Asad in twenty-five minutes, their fastest run ever. The Iraqi prisoner repeatedly asked for water until a few minutes before landing, when Jason's blood-drenched head bandage burst, sending a red cascade through the mesh stretcher and onto the Iraqi's face below. After that the man remained quiet and clenched shut his eyes and mouth.

At about 3:45 p.m. the remnants of Lieutenant Colonel Lopez's reconstituted convoy limped back into base on flat tires and wheel rims. Lopez marched to the trauma tent to check on his men, especially Lance Corporal Falah. Akram basked in the fatherly pride he saw in the colonel's eyes. Ayad, the wounded Iraqi translator, rode back in the most heavily armored Humvee and agreed to let the doctors patch him up. Soon afterward he was evacuated to al Asad and then Baghdad. Somewhere along the way someone wrote on his arm in ink, "I'm an Iraqi-American translator," so he wouldn't accidentally be thrown in with the wounded prisoners. Ayad was still in the hospital when his wife gave birth to their son. He later returned to al Qa'im for a short spell, but his heart was no longer in it. He declined to accompany the Marines on patrols or raids. Over the summer he went to Baghdad on vacation. He didn't return.

By 4 p.m., Lance Corporal Whittenberg's buttock was bleeding badly enough from the shot that had passed through his canteen that Lieutenant Gordinier sent him for medical treatment. Whittenberg, still stinging from his commanders' rebukes over his performance during the ambush, tried to give the lieutenant back a pair of yellow sunglasses he had borrowed. He was glad to hear the lieutenant's response: "You can keep it—you've earned it." At the shock-trauma tent the doctors removed a piece of shrapnel from his rear and gave him a rectal exam to check for bleeding. "You know, I've always had people threaten to rip me a new asshole," Whittenberg joked with the doctors. "But I've never had anyone go through with it before."

At 4:15 p.m. Lieutenant Colonel Lopez allowed the doctors to clean and dress the gunshot wound in his own back.

The attendants loaded Falah, Hampton, Miller, and Lightfoot into litters in the back of a Humvee ambulance and drove them to a landing zone. Inside the ambulance, morphine greased the conversation.

"If I could take the colonel's bullet, I'd take it a million times," Falah informed the other Marines. "I love the colonel."

Pfc. Miller spoke to Hampton on the stretcher above him. "Lance Corporal Hampton?" he began.

"What, Miller?"

"Am I still a boot?"

"No, Miller. Now shut up, Miller."

"Aye, Lance Corporal."

On the helo, Bill Hampton pulled his green camouflage-patterned poncho liner over his head and fell asleep before takeoff.

VII | *The Expectant Ward*

Al Asad, Iraq

ON THE MORNING of April 14, Becky Sparks, commander of Alpha Surgical Company, received an e-mail with new instructions from the chief surgeon of the First Marine Expeditionary Force. The title—Treatment of Expectant Patients—would have struck a civilian as out of place in a hospital in the middle of a combat zone. But in battlefield medicine, "expectant" means quite the opposite of what it does in the faraway world of maternity wards and delivery rooms. An expectant mother is expected to create life. An expectant soldier is expected to die.

"Occasionally, in our triage of patients in the combat environment, we classify patients as 'expectant,' " the chief surgeon wrote.

> With multiple casualties, these patients have our lowest priority for care, but they have the highest priority for care for another member of our Navy/Marine Corps team: the Chaplain.
>
> An "expectant" patient does not always die.

"Expectant" means you expect something to happen, and most often it is death, but sometimes, after the higher priority patients have been treated, an expectant patient survives. Their care should be continued with the resources that can be committed. "Heroic" efforts may seem to be helpful in the short run, but if the resources are expended when the next patient arrives, then you have not helped this latter patient. This is when judgments are critical, and I would dare say that very, very few of us have enough experience to make these decisions easily. When the decisions must be made, talk about it, include your entire team in your decisions, and move on.

If the patient is expectant, make sure that he is comfortable and that someone stays with him until "something" happens. If the patient does die, document the death appropriately.

Alpha Surgical Company had had only one expectant patient up until that time. Plenty of wounded Marines and sailors had passed through the Navy hospital at al Asad air base, with arms shattered by roadside bombs, legs perforated by bullets, or faces torn open by shrapnel. But those fated to die had almost always done so closer to the battlefield, never making it to the more advanced care that Alpha Surgical Company offered. The exception was a Marine shot through the eye in early April. His brains had been spilling from his head; it had taken just a few minutes for him to expire.

At the 7 a.m. staff meeting, Commander Sparks, a brisk woman whose auburn hair and bright lipstick stood out next to the black 9 mm pistol hanging from her shoulder, passed the chief surgeon's message along to her physicians. She briefly discussed it with them, highlighting the advice that doctors revisit the expectant once they have treated the other patients. Then she moved on to other issues.

That afternoon Jason Dunham arrived at Alpha Surgical Company, expected to die.

Located deep in the desert 110 miles west of Baghdad, al Asad seemed far removed from the front. The sprawling base had been one of the jewels of the Iraqi Air Force, with Yugoslav-built concrete bunkers that at one time sheltered the bulk of Saddam's air power and dreams of empire. After Saddam's quick defeat in the Gulf War, the Iraqi Air Force abandoned its long runways, movie theater, and extensive hospital filled with dusty equipment. When Australian special forces troops captured al Asad during the 2003 invasion, they stumbled upon fighter jets still hidden in palm groves, camouflaged in dry riverbeds, and buried in the sand to avoid U.S. air attacks. The Australians handed the base over to the U.S. Army, and on the dirty-white wall of the hospital lobby was a soldier's painting, in shades of gray, of an Army medic kneeling over a fallen comrade.

The Marines took over from the Army in early 2004 and patrolled out of al Asad in Humvee gun trucks and eight-wheeled armored personnel carriers. But the airfield was essentially a rear base. A Marine air wing kept its transport and attack helicopters there, and four-propeller Hercules transport planes, flown by National Guardsmen from West Virginia, Nevada, Rhode Island, and other units, made frequent supply runs to Kuwait. They carried out the flag-covered coffins of those who had died and carried in fresh troops to replace them.

The Americans erected their own comforts and necessities on top of the ruins of the Iraqi Air Force infrastructure. A private company, hired by the Pentagon, brought in entire neighborhoods of prefabricated housing built into white shipping containers, each with blackout window blinds, an air conditioner, a metal wardrobe, and beds with mattresses. Other containers held hot showers and flush toilets. Indian contract workers served meals in a sparkling chow hall, where Diet Cokes, Sprites, and Orange Fantas chilled in the cooler, glass vases with plastic daisies adorned the tables, and CNN news or NBA games blared from big-screen televisions. On the right night, the Marines could eat Cornish hens or T-bone steaks with hot fries. Sunday at al Asad was the flag-football tournament. Monday was darts night. Tuesday was salsa night, with free lessons. Wednesday was three-on-three basketball. Thursday was Old School Night, with music for the over-thirty crowd (IDs required). Friday offered either blackjack or, for the combative, "Friday Night Fights—Open to All Contenders."

The Marine infantrymen at the front, the grunts, had unkind names for those farther back eating Cornish hens and dancing salsa. They might be REMFs, which stood for rear-echelon motherfuckers. Or simply POGs—pronounced "poegues"—probably an acronym for People Other than Grunts. In Iraq it was common to hear the people who were grunts swapping stories and complaints about those who were not. How an occasional mortar round or rocket sent the POGs scurrying to their bunkers, or how the Marines who least needed it had the fancy counterbattery radar, which traced the path of incoming mortar or artillery shells and guided quick retribution back the other way. All Marines shared a sense of superiority toward other services—in the Marines' view, the Air Force was coddled by small luxuries, the Army didn't have enough endurance or discipline, and the Navy tended toward chubbiness. The social hierarchy extended in ever more subtle gradations all the way up to the bayonet's tip. Those posted to the Third Battalion's wildest outpost, Husaybah, felt more pure, more warriorlike, than those even one step back, at al Qa'im.

The Marines at the rear, who were also weaned on the Corps' theology in which glory derives from suffering, knew what the grunts thought of them, and many of the Marines at al Asad wore the slightly guilty looks of those who feel they are too comfortable and too safe. On the wall of an air-conditioned latrine at the base was a blown-up photo of three exhausted grunts sleeping in Fallujah fighting holes that looked like shallow graves. "Think of these Marines the next time you want to complain about life at al Asad," the caption said.

When the war did arrive at al Asad, it usually came by Blackhawk in a rush of stretchers and IV drips. Corporal Dunham's medevac flight happened to land on what turned out to be the worst mass casualty day Alpha Surgical Company had ever seen. The company had six Navy physicians pulled from military hospitals back home: a general surgeon, an ob-gyn surgeon, a family practitioner, a pediatric cardiologist, an internist specializing in cancer, and a psychiatrist. There were two operating rooms, and the facility was designed to provide care for up to three days. Any patients requiring longer or specialized treatment had to go on to Baghdad or Balad.

The pilots of Dunham's Blackhawk floated into their landing, putting the single rear wheel down first, before the two front wheels dropped to the ground. Four bearers carried his litter to the glass doors of the hospital's emergency entrance. Lieutenant Commander Heidi Kraft, a freckled thirty-five-year-old clinical psychologist, drew in a sharp breath when she saw Corporal Dunham arrive, the breathing tube protruding from his mouth and a bloody bandage wrapped around the top of his head. His eyes were swollen shut, but blood was seeping out from underneath the swollen tissue and forming red pools in his eye sockets. The left side of his face appeared badly bruised.

The bearers carried him into the emergency room for triage. In a civilian hospital, triage means helping first those who need it the most. The assumption is that there are enough doctors, nurses, beds, operating rooms, and medications for everyone, and the emergency room staff just has to figure out who is in the most precarious condition. In battlefield medicine, the assumption is that there's only so much treatment available and spending it on soldiers who are likely to die could cost less seriously wounded troops their lives. The military triage team's job is to save the most lives possible by sorting those they will treat from those they won't. Those they don't treat they classify as expectant. It's a Godlike role that ordinary men play.

Commander Jesus Mallari, the fifty-two-year-old pediatric cardiologist, was the duty doctor in the emergency room, assigned the task of stabilizing the patients as they arrived. The nursing staff thought Dr. Mallari a man of few words, almost curt. In fact, the stream of mangled young Marines he had seen since mid-March had left him fragile and struggling to maintain a professional distance from the misery around him. Once he began talking, he couldn't contain his emotions. So he didn't talk much.

Probing gently, he could feel holes on the left side of Jason's skull, and in the confusion concluded he must have been shot in the head. Jason wasn't posturing, the way he had been doing at al Qa'im, and he had begun breathing without the aid of the ventilator bag that had sustained him during the flight. But Dr. Mallari saw no movement that would have indicated the corporal was neurologically intact. The doctors found it troubling that he wasn't "bucking the tube"—gagging or struggling to get the ventilator tube itself out of his throat—and that neither pupil was reacting to light.

Ultimately it was up to the senior surgeon, Commander Tony Villaflor, to decide whether Corporal Dunham would get treatment or just comfort at al Asad. The bespectacled fifty-nine-year-old faced two patients with critical abdominal wounds plus three others in the surgical ward, and he had no neurosurgeon on staff even if he had thought it a good idea to operate on Jason's brain. *This guy's chances of surviving an operation are nil to none,* Dr. Villaflor thought. He consulted with Dr. Tom Gaylord, the ob-gyn surgeon. Dr. Gaylord, a fifty-four-year-old Californian with a bright white crew cut, agreed that the Marine's wounds were mortal, and he was reluctant to risk a helicopter crew to take Corporal Dunham to Baghdad for brain surgery. Nor did he want to be left without a Blackhawk for long, in case another surgical case needed a medevac. Dr. Mallari raised no objections and signed the handwritten medical record: "Dr. Gaylord/Dr. Villaflor examined pt. & determined to be expectant based on massive head injury." When he realized what was happening, Chaplain Alan Lenz, who had been hovering in the background trying to stay out of the way, stepped forward and asked aloud for the Lord to draw near to Corporal Dunham.

In Alpha Surgical Company's contingency plan for dealing with a mass casualty event—shortened to "mass cal" in military lingo—responsibility for the expectant ward fell to the Navy dental team. They had enough general medical knowledge to push intravenous fluids into a dying man, but not enough to be of much use in the trauma ward, operating room, or intensive care unit. Dental Technician First Class Christopher Graham, who had helped carry Jason's stretcher in from the helicopter, had been waiting outside the emergency room while the doctors completed their triage. After fifteen minutes, the door opened and an order emerged from the chaos: "Please take this patient to the expectant ward."

A soulful-eyed thirty-year-old, Graham decorated his barracks room in patriotica. His blanket sported an American flag with a soaring eagle in the center, and the darts stuck into his dartboard had tiny U.S. flags as fins. A photo on the wall showed his daughter standing next to a framed eagle-and-flag print with the caption "These colors don't run." Back home in Lakeside, California, Graham and his wife—a Navy corpsman—perched crossed American flags on top of their Christmas tree, instead of an angel.

Graham and three others carried Corporal Dunham's litter to a dim, white-tiled room with a pair of broken shower stalls. A tape above the door read "Wash Room." All the sawhorses were in use elsewhere, so the litter team carefully placed the stretcher on the floor. Graham sat by the corporal's side, across from Rachael Stirling, a twenty-one-year-old dental technician third class. Stirling had chosen service in the Navy because her grandfather and great-uncle had been sailors. Navy Lieutenant James L. Harris III, a thirty-two-year-old dentist from Crockett, Texas, joined them in the expectant ward, as did the chaplain, Lieutenant Lenz.

Then they waited for Corporal Dunham to die.

For forty-five minutes they spoke to him in soft voices, holding his hands and stroking his limp, muscular arms as Lieutenant Harris pushed fluids and painkillers into his veins from an IV sack. "The Marine Corps is proud of you, and we're all proud of you," Graham told him. Dunham's tattered camouflage fatigues were tucked into his litter, and on his blouse they saw his name patch and the double chevrons of a corporal. Graham wanted to know his first name, however, and went through his pockets in search of an ID. His dog tag just identified him as "J. L. Dunham" and a Methodist, so the sailors were left having to call him Corporal Dunham.

The sailors stared at Jason's skull tattoos, and Christopher Graham and Rachael Stirling passed around the dog tag, wondering what kind of person Corporal Dunham was. Christopher found a folded military-issue map of Iraq, with a few simple Arabic words and phrases, like "Halt" and "I'm an American." He concluded that the corporal must be an exemplary Marine, always prepared with the right gear. Rachael watched Jason's breathing tube, no longer connected to a ventilator bag, fog up when he exhaled, then clear again when he inhaled. At one point he seemed to stop breathing for a few seconds, and the sailors held their breath, too. They felt deeply uneasy; they were neither trauma surgeons nor critical care nurses, but it chafed that they were supposed to sit idle and wait for a badly injured young Marine to expire.

Lieutenant Harris fumed silently about the Iraqis, wondering why the people this Marine had come to help would have done such a thing to him. The chaplain, Lieutenant Lenz, was not one to tell the Lord what to do with his flock. The lieutenant had heard the call to faith while still an enlisted sailor in the late 1970s, and he carried himself with the confidence of a believer. He prayed fervently that God would restore Corporal Dunham's health. But, he added, "if that's not Your will, I commend into Your care this brave Marine's soul."

When the time came to change his IV bag, Heidi Kraft, the psychologist, took over holding Jason's left hand, while Rachael Stirling continued to hold his right. Heidi felt herself immediately drawn to Jason and was unable to let go even after the new bag of fluids was in place above him. She and the dental technicians took turns talking to him, repeating themselves to avoid long silences as they waited for his breathing to become labored and then stop. "Corporal Dunham— we're all here," Heidi said dozens of times. "We're not going to leave you."

At first, Jason's hands were cold and limp, with just the slightest reflexive twitching. But they grew warmer as the minutes ticked by. At one point, Rachael Stirling placed her own hand on his chest and felt the heavy thumping of his heart against his ribs. She thought she sensed an aura of some sort and was sure that he was fighting to survive. Heidi felt his pulse and found it strong and steady. Christopher Graham wondered quietly, *How can this guy be expectant if he's breathing like this?*

They thought Jason looked uncomfortable. His upper body was so large from weight lifting that his arms draped over the sides of the stretcher and down to the floor. They undid the strap across his chest and started to tuck his arms inside. As they did so, Heidi felt Jason squeeze her left hand—not a nervous twitch, but a strong, distinct compression. His biceps and forearm flexed at the same time.

"Oh my God," she said, looking up. "He just squeezed my hand."

"Corporal, can you hear me?" she asked urgently. This time Jason squeezed Heidi Kraft's hand and pulled her down close to his chest. Heidi's voice rose with excitement, and she and the others laughed aloud as Jason repeated the movement over and over.

Commander Sparks, who had been in and out of the expectant ward all afternoon, may have been in charge of Alpha Surgical Company, but she was a lab technologist, not a physician. She felt a layman's reluctance to tell doctors they may have missed something. In Corporal Dunham's case, however, she felt the situation had changed since he had been carried off the helicopter and shuttled to the wash room. She found the physicians gathered at the emergency room. "I never try to tell you how to practice medicine," she told them. "But you know this fellow's heartbeat is strong, he's grasping our hands and holding them. I just think we need to give him another look and see if there's something we can do for him."

Dr. Gaylord initially thought Commander Sparks might have been taking the chief surgeon's memo about expectant patients too seriously, and he was dubious that the Marine was worth treating. The flow of new casualties had reached a lull, however, and the doctors decamped to the expectant ward. "He's been squeezing my hand in response to our voices," Heidi Kraft told them.

Dr. Mike Danforth, the hospital's family practitioner, put a stethoscope to Dunham's chest, then looked up. "I've got seventy-two beats per minute," he said. Captain Gary Sladek, an oncologist on his twilight tour before retiring from the military, gently pried open Dunham's eyes and shined a light in. The corporal's left pupil remained large and fixed in a blank stare. But his right pupil shrank from the light, and he jerked his head to the side. Again he yanked Heidi toward him. She and the dental team cheered giddily.

At 5:20 p.m. Dr. Danforth ordered Corporal Dunham taken to the intensive care unit and readied for a medevac to the Thirty-first Combat Support Hospital in Baghdad. Graham and the others picked up Jason's litter and carried him out of the expectant ward.

The ICU at al Asad was a simple affair, a white room with speckled tiles on the floor and silver blankets covering the windows. Patients rested on olive drab army cots, with bright orange padding for comfort and sterility. The only other patient on the cots when Jason arrived was the Iraqi prisoner, whose chest wounds had been complicated by hemorrhaging in his abdominal cavity. His ankles were still bound in plastic flexicuffs, and twenty-year-old Lance Corporal Clinton Noel stood guard over the Iraqi with his M16, a round loaded into the firing chamber. Noel had wanted to be a Marine since the ninth grade; he had to fight back the urge to "fucking blow the guy away" where he lay.

Ensign Karen Lovecchio, a twenty-five-year-old nurse from New Jersey, had been caring for the Iraqi POW. His vital signs were unstable, but Karen's own pulse didn't twitch when his blood pressure or oxygen set off the monitor alarms. When Dunham's litter arrived in the ICU, she simply turned away from the Iraqi and devoted herself to the Marine. Karen, who wore her brown hair pulled back to expose a high forehead, held the key to the narcotics cabinet and had been to the expectant ward a couple of times to give Jason morphine. On one of those visits he had squeezed her hand, sending shivers down her spine.

Karen knew that Corporal Dunham had been especially responsive to Heidi Kraft, so she ordered the psychologist, several ranks her senior, to put on sterile latex gloves and continue to keep the Marine company while they waited for the medevac helicopter. Heidi was thrilled to be included, and she laughed aloud when he grasped her hand. She even thought he moved his head and toes on command. The ICU staff exchanged smiles when their eyes met. Chaplain Lenz came into the room, and Heidi told him she thought they needed a different prayer. This time the chaplain prayed for safety on the flight and for divine guidance for the medical staff in Baghdad.

Heidi realized she wouldn't be allowed to accompany Jason on the Blackhawk to Baghdad, so she introduced him to Navy Lieutenant Steve Noakes, a thirty-eight-year-old physician's assistant. Steve used to do search-and-rescue work in California, rappelling from helicopters to rescue downed pilots, hang gliders, and other unfortunate adventurers. "In a minute I'm going to have to let go of your hand," Heidi told Jason. "But that's O.K. because my friend Steve will take over."

Dunham was urinating freely through a catheter, which the nurses interpreted as a good sign. They elevated his head and hooked his breathing tube back up to the ventilator. Steve injected mannitol, a sugary drug to control brain in-flammation, into Jason's intravenous drip. Karen and Heidi held his hands and wiped his battered face. Karen thought about Corporal Dunham's parents, waking up in the United

States and heading off to work, unaware that their son lay bleeding in an Iraqi hospital.

The more attached they grew to Corporal Dunham, the more embittered the medical team grew about having to treat the wounded Iraqi on the next cot. Medical ethics and the rules of land warfare dictated that they provide him the best of care. But they suspected the POW had had something to do with the incident that left the Marine so critically wounded. Karen Lovecchio played a mental game with herself and decided that once she was looking after Corporal Dunham, she didn't care what happened to the Iraqi. Lieutenant (junior grade) Katie Foster, who had been Jason's nurse in the emergency room when he arrived at al Asad a couple of hours earlier, had been angry to see an Iraqi fighter receiving treatment while an American was being carted off to the expectant ward. Nonetheless, Katie stepped in when she saw that Dunham's arrival at the ICU had left the Iraqi unattended. At first the Iraqi had just moaned and asked for water. Later, however, he seemed to flirt with the blue-eyed twenty-three-year-old. As he was being carted away to the operating room, he smiled up at her and said in English, "I love you." Then he smacked his lips in a faux kiss. Katie took it as a facetious gesture and felt a rising fury battling with her sense of duty. She decided on a compromise: she wouldn't hold his hand, but she would speak to him in as reassuring a way as she could muster. When the Iraqi was thirsty, he got water. When he complained that his head hurt, he got a pillow. At one point he began to pee blood through his catheter; at another the IV needle ripped the vein and his arm bloated up with fluid.

When the ICU team heard the Blackhawk approach, they

strapped Jason to his stretcher and carried him into the hall. Dozens of people watched as he passed through the glass emergency room doors. Steve Noakes had reattached the manual ventilator bag and walked alongside the litter, breathing for the corporal. Heidi Kraft held Jason's hand, assuring him that the doctors and nurses in Baghdad would take good care of him. She said how proud she was of him for fighting and promised never to forget him. She was riding a manic high, her voice reflecting her new hopes for his survival. On the pathway to the helipad, Jason gripped Heidi so hard that she had to peel his hand away.

After the Blackhawk left, Dr. Villaflor operated on the Iraqi while Lance Corporal Noel, the security guard, watched wearing a blue surgical mask and carrying his rifle. The Marine's presence was mostly to satisfy personal curiosity, since the prisoner was unconscious. The doctor cut the Iraqi open from the sternum to the abdomen, picking out bone chips and trying to figure out why he was bleeding internally. The surgeon pulled out the Iraqi's intestines and described various organs for Noel's benefit. Afterward, he sewed the man up and, that evening, sent him to the big U.S. airbase in Balad, north of Baghdad, for further treatment. The doctor feared, however, that the prisoner was already too far gone to survive, that he, too, would soon be expectant.

When the work slowed, Captain Sladek, the oncologist, was still thinking about the decision to put Corporal Dunham in the expectant ward. He knocked on Commander Becky Sparks's office door, the back of which was covered with greeting-card photos of kittens. Sparks insisted on sleeping in her office on a bed made of two-by-fours so she'd hear the sound of incoming Blackhawks. "I'm glad you came to get us," Dr. Sladek told her.

Karen Lovecchio kept a journal in a blue-and-gold silk-bound notebook that her boyfriend had made. Her writing revealed a woman mourning the dead and mutilated boys, while wondering whether anything in her future would ever compare to the sense of purpose and intensity she had found in Iraq at the age of twenty-five. "They lay there so helpless and it's my job (and the docs') to piece them back together," she wrote. "This whole experience is so much more than I expected (good and bad)." Among her musings she glued photos of the Philadelphia Flyers hockey team and headlines clipped from the *Stars and Stripes* newspaper. "21 Dead in Two Days of Unrest in Iraq." "5 Marines Killed in Ambush Near Syria." "Bloody Day in Iraq." On April 15 she wrote: "I wonder how much longer it can go on like this with Marines dying left and right—it's so sad." But she also wrote a letter to her boyfriend about the "Miracle Marine" who had survived the expectant ward.

Katie Foster was less optimistic. When Corporal Dunham left for Baghdad, her heart and her head told her that he wouldn't live. She just hoped he would get home so his family could say good-bye.

Heidi Kraft couldn't shake the memory of the strong young Marine pulling on her hand, clinging to her as they parted. She looked back at her few hours with Corporal Dunham as a spiritual awakening that explained why she was in Iraq at all. "The litter team loaded him in the bird and it took off," she wrote to her family.

I stood there, frozen, watching the cloud of dust rise and the huge propeller lift them into the sky. They were joined by their attack helicopter escort, and together they made the turn and disappeared. I turned around. A large group of people had gathered around this remarkable patient and stood in quiet awe. The rest of the patients were either in surgery or on the ward. We could stop for a moment. I was aware then of my body, trembling at my knees, and I raised shaky hands to my face, without realizing I still had my gloves on. And then the tears came.

VIII | *Brain Surgery*

Baghdad, Iraq

STEVE NOAKES HAD promised Heidi Kraft that he'd talk to Corporal Dunham on the way to Baghdad, but the deep *thwap-thwap-thwap* of the helicopter blades made conversation—even a one-sided conversation—almost impossible aboard the Black-hawk. "Hang in there," Steve yelled. "You're almost there." Every three seconds during the forty-five-minute flight, Steve squeezed the plastic ventilator bag to force air into Jason's lungs, changing hands when he cramped up. Blood continued to pool in the corporal's left eye and ran down the side of his face to his ear. Steve couldn't help thinking it looked like a tear.

The helicopter touched down at 6:50 p.m. on the faded red cross of the tarmac landing pad, where medics waited with a metal rickshaw built on two spoked wheels. They fixed Corporal Dunham's stretcher onto the frame and rolled him a hundred feet down the street into the courtyard of what used to be Saddam Hussein's personal hospital, where an Iraqi man named Samir with a big Saddam mustache now sold bread and eggs to the U.S. troops and laundered military uniforms for five dollars a sack under a trellis of plastic hibiscus flowers.

Such tiny stores sprang up at U.S. camps, checkpoints, and hospitals all over Iraq, anywhere local entrepreneurs could get close enough to the wealthy Americans. The troops called them "hajji shops." When they had stormed into Iraq a year earlier, the Marines and soldiers had used "hajjis" as a slur for Iraqis, much like the krauts, Japs, and gooks of wars past. The practice receded after the troops learned enough rudimentary Arabic to realize that hajji wasn't as insulting as they had hoped; it was actually a title of respect for a Muslim who had made the sacred pilgrimage to Mecca. Nonetheless, hajji shop remained part of the military vernacular, and Baghdad's Green Zone was sprinkled with them.

The Green Zone covered roughly four square miles of monolithic palaces, wide boulevards, oversized monuments, and wandering waterways on the western side of the Tigris River, which meandered through the middle of Baghdad. During Saddam's reign, the area had been largely closed to ordinary Iraqis, a place of mystery, rumor, and danger. Many Iraqis drove far out of their way just to avoid the risk of breaking down and attracting attention in front of Saddam's guards. Ibn Sina Hospital was the finest in Iraq, solely for the care of Saddam's inner circle. Ibn Sina himself was a revered Muslim physician, theologian, and philosopher who, in the eleventh century, had cured a Persian ruler of colic and been made vizier in return. Saddam reportedly brought foreign doctors to Ibn Sina Hospital in 1996 to treat his famously sadistic son, Uday, after two gunmen in tracksuits sprayed him with bullets. The hospital's radiology department boasted the latest diagnostic equipment, including a doughnut-shaped German computerized tomography (CT) scanner and an advanced magnetic resonance imaging (MRI) system.

As Saddam's regime fell in April 2003, thousands of Iraqis

rushed into the Green Zone in an orgy of joy and revenge. They pillaged palaces and offices and squatted in the homes once reserved for Saddam's family and Baath Party officials. They ignited government buildings, turning Baghdad's sky-line into a smear of black smoke. They ransacked Ibn Sina, apparently leaving behind the CT scanner and MRI only be-cause the machines were too large to fit through the door. Fighting their way into the capital, U.S. troops, including the Marine battalion that Corporal Dunham would later join, stood aside and shook their heads in amazement as men, women, and children made off with new motorcycles and electric generators on stolen hydraulic lifts. Looters carried away computers in donkey carts and, impervious to irony, walked away with kitchen sinks.

The U.S.-led occupying authority quickly seized the Green Zone as its own protected haven, installing Army sergeants in apartments and civilian bureaucrats in palaces. American soldiers in helmets and flak vests posed for souvenir snapshots under the giant swords that arched across the boulevard near Iraq's Tomb of the Unknown Soldier monu-ment. The coalition held press conferences touting the suc-cesses of the occupation in a convention center decorated with tilework depicting the defeat of American forces. Ibn Sina became a U.S. Army hospital and, as the initial glee of liberation gave way to a guerrilla uprising, a sanctuary for wounded Americans funneled in from field hospitals around Iraq for passage home.

When Corporal Dunham arrived at Ibn Sina, the sign outside the emergency room entrance identified it as the new home of the Thirty-first Combat Support Hospital, a unit based at Fort Bliss, Texas, near the Mexican border. If April 14 was busy for the doctors at al Asad, the funneling effect made it even more frenzied at the 31st CSH—pronounced "cash"—which received patients from across the hostile Sunni Muslim areas where the anticoalition insurgency was most violent. The emergency room saw sixty-seven casualties that day, fifty-two of them U.S. troops. Any soldier or Marine with a head wound ended up at the 31st CSH in Baghdad because the hospital had the only two military neurosurgeons in the whole theater of operations. In the trauma ward, Steve Noakes met one of them, Lieutenant Colonel Jeff Poffenbarger, the chief of the neurosurgery team, and almost apologetically explained that Corporal Dunham had been plucked from the expectant ward back in al Asad.

"We thought this guy was dead, and he's not."

If a soldier is lucky enough to survive the bleeding and shock of a head wound, he still faces two principal dangers: First, the shrapnel or bullet itself kills the tissue it hits and can leave the brain so badly damaged that the wounded man might lose his ability to walk, talk, understand, or even breathe. Second, the injury can cause the brain to swell. Neurosurgeons are fond of saying that the brain is locked in a closed vault. What they mean is that the brain, normally a good fit inside the skull, has only so much room to expand before it bumps up against the cranium. The analogy isn't quite right, however; the vault has one hole. At the base of the skull is a walnut-sized opening called the foramen magnum, where the brain stem meets the spinal column. If the brain swells too much, its only escape route is down through the foramen magnum, a condition called herniation. Herniation crushes and kills the cells in the brain stem, which control the involuntary basics of life, such as breathing and heart rate.

One way neurosurgeons assess the damage from a head wound is to score the patient on the Glasgow Coma Scale. The patient gets points in three categories: eye opening, motor response, and verbal response. A normal, uninjured person would get the maximum score of 15: 4 points for spontaneously opening his eyes, 6 points for holding up the right number of fingers when told to do so, and 5 points for conversing coherently. Someone in a light coma might get 9 points: 2 for opening his eyes in response to pain, 4 for pulling away in response to a pinch on the neck, and 3 for speaking but using inappropriate words. Someone in the very deepest coma, unresponsive to any stimulus, would still get a total score of 3. When Jason arrived at Alpha Surgical Company in al Asad, he scored a 3.

In the trauma ward, Jeff Poffenbarger conducted a quick test to see how much neurological damage Jason had sustained. The doctor rubbed his knuckle sharply on Jason's chest. Jason winced and pulled his arms upward toward his chin, hands curled and facing inward toward each other. It was the same posturing that had worried the doctors in the shock-trauma tent back in al Qa'im. The doctors in the field had been right—posturing wasn't a good sign. But, given Jason's extensive injury, it was better than not responding at all. Dr. Poffenbarger gave him 3 points for motor response.

He pried open Jason's swollen eyes and shined a light in. Jason's left pupil measured six millimeters across and didn't flinch when the light hit it. His right pupil measured four millimeters, and shrank away from the light. Jason got just 1 point on his coma score, the least possible, for eye movement; after all, he didn't open his eyes on his own. But the pupils told Dr. Poffenbarger that the damage, while serious, wasn't necessarily fatal. If both pupils had been "blown"—in other words, completely dilated and unresponsive to light—it would have been a sign of damage so severe that Jason would have had virtually no chance of recovering enough to have a meaningful life. Pupils that are small and respond to light are at least evidence that synapses are still firing inside the brain. And Jason's pupil response marked a surprising improvement from what it had been when he landed at al Asad, where his left pupil had been frozen open at ten millimeters and his right pupil fixed at two millimeters.

Watching the exam from the foot of the bed, Steve Noakes told Dr. Poffenbarger that Jason had responded to voices at Alpha Surgical Company. Dr. Poffenbarger gave Steve a dubious look, then leaned down and said something to Jason. Jason squeezed the doctor's hand—a good sign but not enough to constitute a full response to verbal commands. The neurosurgeons knew that hand squeezing could be a very primitive reflex and might not have anything to do with consciousness. To get extra coma points Jason would have had to hold up two fingers or give a thumbs-up sign, either motion unambiguous evidence that he understood a command. Jason got 1 point for verbal response, for a total coma score of 5. The last thing Steve remembered seeing before he walked back out to the Blackhawk was Dr. Poffenbarger looking up at him from Jason's side and nodding, as if to confirm that something in Jason was indeed fighting for life.

In a civilian trauma center in the United States, 95 percent of patients with coma scores of 5 or less died from their injuries or wound up in a vegetative state. But those odds clumped together crack addicts with gunshot wounds, elderly people with fragile immune systems, and the rest of the rainbow of humankind. The troops in Iraq were generally far younger and healthier than the American population as a whole, with a lot more resilience in their brains than older patients. Back in San Antonio, where Dr. Poffenbarger's 359th Neurosurgical Detachment was based, a junkie with a head wound and a coma score of 5 probably wouldn't have been deemed a candidate for surgery. But as long as the emergency room wasn't too full, a coma score of 5 and a single reactive pupil were enough to get a Marine a chance on the operating table at the 31st CSH.

Between them, the two neurosurgeons at the 31st CSH opened 110 craniums during the first five months they were in Iraq. The fast-talking Major Richard Gullick bore more than a passing resemblance to the portly comedian Jon Lovitz. Fueled by diet cola, the thirty-six-year-old shuffled around the hospital halls in green clogs and surgical scrub caps that his mother stitched from fabric decorated in soaring eagles and American flags. An intense, slender, bespectacled man, the forty-one-year-old Dr. Poffenbarger had himself been a grunt with the Army Rangers and Green Berets before taking up brain surgery. He joked that the team's motto could be, "If you take a round to the skull from Damascus to Teheran, Diyarbakir to Kuwait City, you come see us."

The surgeons had a repertoire of stories about the random kindness and cruelty of war, of patients who should have lived and didn't, patients who shouldn't have lived and did. Rich Gullick treated one U.S. soldier with both an abdominal wound and a glancing blow to the skull. He arrived at the hospital with a coma score of 3—the same score the examining table itself would have gotten had anyone bothered to test it. Within a couple of days he was well enough to talk to his wife on the phone. Jeff Poffenbarger treated a soldier who had been hit by a bullet that went through the cartilage in his right ear, bounced off the skull behind it, turned south and

lodged point-down in his neck. Jeff attributed the soldier's
survival to bad Iraqi ammunition. The round just didn't have
enough momentum to penetrate the bone. The neurosurgeons were particularly fond of the story of Lance Corporal
Sterling "Rooster" Bucholz, a machine gunner from New
Mexico who was shot in the helmet and survived. The first
shot apparently skipped off his Kevlar helmet; Rooster was
never quite sure. But the second bullet penetrated the Kevlar
itself, ricocheted off Rooster's skull, and hit the helmet again
farther back, creating a small blister in the surface of the helmet before running out of steam. Rooster was briefly paralyzed and blinded, but Rich Gullick repaired a six-inch scalp
laceration, relieved the bruising beneath his skull, and installed a pair of titanium plates to patch the cracks. By the end
of the month the only remaining damage was a lack of coor-
dination in Rooster's left arm, which doctors predicted
would recede with physical therapy. Rooster kept the helmet.

The long parade of men with head wounds had left Dr.
Poffenbarger obsessed with helmets. He kept a small collection of battle-damaged headgear on a dented metal shelf outside the operating room. The classic steel-pot helmet so
evocative of Normandy, the Chosin Reservoir, and Hue City
didn't stop the 7.62 mm rounds fired from an AK-47 assault
rifle. During the 1983 U.S. invasion of the tiny Caribbean island of Grenada, the Army had its first chance to test in combat a new kind of helmet made of Kevlar, a tightly woven
fabric that absorbed the impact of flying metal. The brief war
also produced the first documented case of a hostile AK
round failing to penetrate an American helmet with a direct
shot. The Kevlars were bulky, weighed more than four
pounds, and bore an uncomfortable resemblance to Wer-
macht helmets from Nazi Germany. But they offered far

more protection than the steel pots, and in Iraq the troops quickly became religious about wearing them.

The combination of American body armor and Iraqi guerrilla tactics had changed the nature of combat wounds. Because the American troops wore hardened ceramic plates in the front and back of their flak vests, lethal sucking chest wounds and abdominal wounds made up a far smaller share of injuries than they had in wars past. On the Iraqi side, insurgents increasingly shied away from gunfights with American troops and instead resorted to planting roadside bombs made of mortar rounds, artillery shells, or rockets, often set off remotely by invisible hands as U.S. convoys or patrols passed. Such weapons, like hand grenades, sprayed rocks, dirt, and shards of jagged metal at 1,000 feet per second, usually upward and outward in a fountain pattern. The result was that military doctors saw many shrapnel wounds to the arms and legs and to the areas of the head exposed to a blast from below. Frequently the surgeons at the 31st CSH heard a boom from some corner of Baghdad and within fifteen minutes found themselves with a ward full of bloody new patients. In the rush of casualties on the evening of April 14, Poffenbarger and Gullick had no idea that Dunham had been injured trying to absorb the blast of a hand grenade. His records from the 31st CSH said he had been hit in an ambush with an improvised explosive device, the military term for a roadside bomb.

During World War II and even to a degree in Vietnam almost all soldiers with serious head injuries were considered expectant. But military surgeons had learned a great deal since Vietnam, particularly from Israel's experience during the 1982 invasion of Lebanon. The Israelis had an advanced neurosurgical center in Haifa close to the Lebanese border and were able to get wounded soldiers quickly into the hands of specialists. The Israeli doctors found they got good results by being intentionally less aggressive than surgeons had been in Korea and Vietnam about removing deeply embedded metal and bone fragments.

Dr. Gullick, who treated Jason, also had the advantage of having Saddam Hussein's CT scanner on hand to reveal the extent of the swelling in Jason's brain and the location of shrapnel. The scanner took pictures of horizontal slices of the inside of Jason's head, as seen from below. Normally, there's a visible line that divides the brain into right and left halves. In Jason's head, the left side of the brain was badly bruised and so swollen that the line bowed into the right half. And Jason already showed signs of herniating; his temporal lobe was pressing hard on his brain stem. But the herniation was not so severe that the surgeons thought it was beyond repair, and Jason's blood pressure and heartbeat were stable.

Rich Gullick's job was to remove dead brain tissue, and to relieve the pressure that was mounting in Jason's head so he wouldn't suffer a fatal brain-stem herniation. At 8:50 p.m. on the day Jason was wounded, Dr. Gullick peeled back the skin on the left side of his head. He then took an electric drill with an acorn-shaped bit and began sinking holes into the hard outer layer of skull, through the blood-filled marrow, and down until only an eggshell-thin layer of bone remained between the outside air and the brain. He then used a small spoonlike tool to flick away the remaining bone in each hole and inserted a special drill that vaguely resembled the foot-and-needle assembly of a sewing machine. The bit sawed through the skull as he maneuvered it sideways. The special foot moved beneath the bit in the space between Jason's brain and the inside of his skull, preventing the bit from accidentally cutting into the brain itself. By connecting the starter holes he had drilled, Dr. Gullick cut loose a curved, football-shaped section of skull from the left side of Jason's head. He lifted off the piece of skull—called the bone flap—and exposed the injured brain below.

Dr. Gullick gently removed loose bone fragments, the residue of the shrapnel's forced entry. Then he poked a suction tool into the wound itself and removed eight or ten tablespoons of dead, purplish-black brain until he exposed the living salmon-and-white brain below. It was hazardous work, done by both sight and feel. The dead brain had the loose consistency of milk curds. The living brain was much firmer to the suction tool's touch. The biggest piece of shrapnel, measuring about a third of an inch by a fifth of an inch, had hit behind Jason's left eye and cut an upward path into his brain, coming to rest three inches in toward the top rear of his skull. Dr. Gullick made no effort to dig the fragment out. Generally, superheated metal shrapnel is sterile and poses little infection danger. On the other hand, rooting around that far inside the brain could cause untold damage and simply wasn't worth the risk, he felt. Four other tiny fragments were lodged in Jason's head—two in his sinuses, one in the front left part of his brain, and one in the left side of his face. But it was the big piece that was endangering his life.

Dr. Gullick then faced a critical choice: he could reattach the bone and close up Jason's skull, or he could leave the bone flap off to prevent the intracranial pressure from building up again. Dr. Poffenbarger, in particular, almost always left the bone flaps off his patients as a precaution; it was very unlikely that a patient would herniate with his skull open on top. He would usually stitch the bone into the patient's abdomen, where the blood flow would keep the bone alive un-

til it was reattached at some later date. If the bone flap was
too contaminated from the injury, doctors could always put
in titanium plates later to cover the gap in the skull. But with
Jason's bone flap and dead tissue removed, Dr. Gullick saw his
brain pull back into his cranium, a promising sign. So Rich
put the flap back on and attached it with three small titanium
covers, held in place with minuscule screws. He also inserted
through Jason's skull a device that resembled a meat ther-
mometer to read his intracranial pressure. A healthy person
usually has a pressure reading of around 10 millimeters of
mercury, with spikes up to 50 or 60 during the instant of a
sneeze. A particularly reluctant bowel movement might drive
someone's intracranial pressure up to 25 for a few seconds. In
a patient in Jason's condition, a sustained reading in the
twenties could be a warning flag for imminent fatal herniation. To be extra cautious, Dr. Gullick had drilled a series of
small holes in the bone flap as safety valves before he put it
back in place. If the swelling worsened, cerebrospinal fluid
could leak out through the holes.

The whole operation took two hours and fifteen minutes,
and Rich Gullick was pleased with the results. The initial intracranial pressure readings were less than 3 millimeters, and
some even dipped into negative numbers, probably a short-
term effect of the monitor's proximity to the suction from
the drain that Dr. Gullick had inserted as well. Rich believed
he had reversed the initial brain-stem herniation in time, and
he expected Jason to survive. What he didn't know was how
much damage the shrapnel and swelling might have already
caused to Jason's brain. Doctors have a good general sense of
what part of the brain controls what aspect of human life. But
they aren't sure exactly what functions they are scraping away
when they remove dead brain tissue. Dr. Gullick guessed that

Jason would lose movement in his right arm and perhaps the side of his face. But would he lose his ability to speak? To assemble the sounds he heard into words that made sense to him? Would he lose his easy smile? His ability to love? Rich didn't know how much of Jason would be left.

———

Just after 11:30 p.m., the medical team pushed Jason's litter into the elevator and up to the second floor of Ibn Sina Hospital. They rolled him down the hall over a strip of orange reflective tape with the word DETAINEE written across it in black capital letters. Behind the tape was a room filled with despondent-looking wounded Iraqi prisoners, and up the small ramp beyond that was Intensive Care Unit 2. The main room of ICU 2 had four beds, pale yellow walls, and a terrazzo tile floor with large chunks of gray and white marble embedded for a patio look. The two windows were crisscrossed with clear medical tape to prevent shattering in case a mortar or rocket landed by the orange tree outside.

Nurses in the regular wards at the 31st CSH daily faced young men, and sometimes young women, with horrific wounds twisting their bodies and minds. But once those patients made it to Baghdad, they rarely died. The ICU was different. The nurses there saw patients whose grasp on life was still tenuous, or whose minds had shut down even if their bodies had not. Jason moved into Bed No. 1 during the bloodiest month the intensive care team had seen in Iraq. If an ICU patient died, the nurses just had time to remove the body and change the sheets before a new patient arrived to take his place. It was an onslaught of stress and sadness that left each member of the ICU team struggling for ways to cope.

The hospital chaplain, Captain Dawud Agbere, often slept in his office, just around the corner from the ICU. A thirty-six-year-old Muslim born in Ghana, he kept on his desk a green, leather-bound copy of the Koran, with gold-embossed Arabic script. Agbere had been an enlisted sailor in the U.S. Navy, but was no great fan of the sea and the Army offered him a chance at a commission in the chaplains' service. He had studied education and Islam in Sudan, Arabic and political science in Ghana, and done graduate work at the Graduate School of Islamic and Social Sciences, a Leesburg, Virginia, institution that turned out many of the military's Muslim chaplains. On his right collar tab were the double bars of a captain; on his left was a brown crescent of Islam. A string of thirty-three black-and-white prayer beads sat on his desk to help him keep count when he observed the Muslim tradition of praising Allah ninety-nine times. He prayed so often, however, that he didn't really need the beads to keep track.

On April 15, Captain Agbere walked to Jason's bedside. When ministering to patients on ventilators, he usually stood by their beds, his hands locked behind his back, and prayed silently in Arabic: "Allah forgive him and have mercy on him." Then he'd add in English, "God, we pray for a speedy recovery." When he prayed over the dead, he'd place his hand on the soldier's head. Later he'd add the man's name to a list of the fallen he kept in a small green notebook, so the dead wouldn't be forgotten. Sergeant X "died of head injuries from an IED attack." Specialist Y arrived "expectant."

The war took Marisol Meléndez Garcia's sleep away. She often couldn't fall asleep, and, when she did, she couldn't stay asleep. She survived for months on coffee and one, two, or, if she was lucky, three hours of sleep a night. A medical-surgical

nurse from Canovanas, Puerto Rico, First Lieutenant Meléndez retained a strong hint of her native accent. She had kind
brown eyes and wore her hair pulled back in a small bun. A
coiled black telephone cord secured her pistol to her right hip.
At thirty-four, she had no children of her own, but she kept
close tabs on her fourteen nieces and nephews, alternately
spoiling them with their favorite gifts and warning them about
the dangers of lying, truancy, and unprotected sex.

Marisol Meléndez remembered bits and pieces of each patient she treated, snapshots of their time together. There was
her first intensive care patient, a soldier with a head wound.
The doctor had warned her that if the soldier's intracranial
pressure rose above 20, he could die. Marisol was so nervous
that she wouldn't allow the cleaning staff near his bed. By ex-
perimenting gingerly, she figured out that his pressure would
drop if she lowered the angle of the head of his bed from the
standard thirty degrees to fifteen degrees. There was the Marine who arrived in a deep coma but improved so quickly
that he could soon breathe without the ventilator. When he
began speaking again, however, he was unable to distinguish
what he had already said from what he wanted to say. He'd
ask for water over and over, even when he had some in his
hand. "My head hurts, my head hurts, my head hurts," he
would chant. When the Marine left the ICU, Lieutenant
Meléndez had everyone working in the ward autograph his
sweat socks, a whim that soon became tradition. The nurses
once drew a six-pack of abdominal muscles on a patient with
a broken spine who was wearing a cast from the chest down.
If a comatose man arrived at a hospital in Germany or Maryland or California with a smiley face on his foot, everyone
knew he had passed through the ICU of the 31st CSH in
Baghdad. If the soldier ever woke up again, he'd have a sou-

venir of someone he had never met, but who had washed him tenderly and held his hand hour after hour.

The Baghdad ICU was an unhealthy place to get healthy. Iraq was home to especially malevolent bacteria, *Acinetobacter baumannii*, and the nurses were eager to get Jason stable enough to travel to Germany. Their main concern in the meantime was to make sure his intracranial pressure remained within an acceptable range. The question was not only whether his pressure readings spiked, but also how quickly they would drop again in response to the range of treatments the nurses and doctors had at their disposal.

Lieutenant Meléndez was working the 7 a.m. to 7 p.m. shift on April 16 when she noticed Jason's intracranial pressure reading jump to 27. Dr. Gullick had left standing orders in case of an ICP spike: she made sure his head and neck, supported by a stiff collar, were aligned with his body, not tilted to the side. She made sure the head of his bed was elevated to thirty degrees. She gave him doses of the sedative thiopental at noon, at 1 p.m., and at 2 p.m. None of it had any effect. His temperature was 101.4 degrees Fahrenheit, and she suspected the fever was causing the increase in pressure in his head. A Tylenol suppository didn't work, nor did placing ice bags under his armpits and scrotum.

"Jason, buddy, help me out," she pleaded. "You have to bring your temperature down." Marisol always called him by his first name because that's what she would have liked had she been the one lying in a coma in a strange land. She also thought she'd like a cool rag on her forehead if she were in Jason's place and had a fevered headache. She walked downstairs to the hospital lab and filled some bags with ice cubes. Back in the ICU, she put the ice into a blue bucket and topped it off with water, then dipped a washcloth into the water and placed it on Jason's forehead, just beneath his gauzy white head bandage. Within seconds, she could see his intracranial pressure fall—27, 26, 25. She was relieved, until she watched it climb right back up as the cloth warmed up. So the next time she placed the chilled cloth on his chest. Again his brain pressure ticked downward, but now it stayed down. Every minute or so she'd repeat the process: dunk the washcloth, place it on his chest, watch the pressure monitor. When the monitor read 11, Marisol sat down next to the bed. She held Jason's hand, let her forehead slump to the mattress by his side, and fell easily asleep.

She slept there for about half an hour and woke up when the low-battery alarm beeped on the IV pump. She looked up at the intracranial pressure monitor. It read 7. "Good job, Jason," she said. When Captain Marvetta Walker arrived for the overnight shift, Lieutenant Meléndez reported on the corporal's progress. "He had a temperature, and the ICP was really high," she said. "The only thing that worked was a really cold washcloth. Either that or he enjoys sleeping with his nurse."

Captain Walker, a thirty-nine-year-old Chicagoan with café-au-lait skin and short, back-swept brown hair tinged in gold, led the line dances at the hospital barbecues and talked of scriptures. One of her own babies had died a few hours after birth, and she found the suffering of her intensive care patients could be too much to handle unless she shut them out of her thoughts when she left the ward. Sometimes she chose not to remember their faces after they left Baghdad.

Marvetta had been on night duty when Jason arrived at the ICU, and she long remembered the way his intracranial pressure would climb, then drop again. But what struck her the most was the clear, light-yellow fluid flowing from his ears. The grenade's concussion had burst Jason's eardrums and allowed cerebrospinal fluid to escape. Marvetta put gauze and a specimen cup under each ear to catch the runoff. The cups held four and a half ounces each, and each ear would fill one cup every couple of hours. She reported the leakage to the doctors, who felt it wasn't necessarily a bad thing. The holes in Jason's ears helped control the pressure inside his head. But the exposure also raised the chances of him picking up an infection.

The night of April 16, Captain Walker turned off Jason's supply of sedatives so the doctors could conduct an accurate neurological exam. Jason's arms moved in response to pain, and he gagged over the breathing tube. But, Marvetta noted in his record, Corporal Dunham "hasn't performed any purposeful movement." Dr. Gullick gave him a coma score of 4, but wasn't worried that his score had fallen. It was common for coma scores to fluctuate after surgery. Jason's left pupil measured six millimeters and remained nonreactive. His right pupil measured three millimeters and still reacted to light. The pupils hinted at a damaged brain, but not one beyond saving.

First Lieutenant Freida Bradshaw was on duty at Jason's bedside the night of April 17 to prepare him for medevac to Germany. At times Freida, a petite critical care nurse from Bastrop, Louisiana, was overwhelmed by the sight of so many broken young men. Though thirty-two years old, she still looked like a teenager herself, and she'd often slip into the supply room or the staff lounge to sob. She gathered up several days' worth of medications for Jason, in case the helicopter went down or just got stuck somewhere. She dressed him in a paper gown, put a folded blanket under his bandaged head, and wrapped him in green army blankets to make what she called a "human burrito shell." He was attached to a portable ventilator, as well as a toaster-sized machine that monitored his heart rate, blood pressure, blood oxygenation, breathing, and temperature. She gave Jason a heavy dose of sedatives and stuffed a few extra syringes in her own pockets for emergency boosters.

Just five-foot-one, she asked the helo crew to put Jason on the bottom rack so she could easily reach him. Usually the nurses would insert foam plugs in their patients' ears to dull the noise of the Blackhawk. But Jason's ears were still leaking cerebrospinal fluid. She didn't put them in her own ears either because, even in the din of the helo, she didn't want to risk missing an alarm from the monitors. The helicopter flew with all its lights out, so Freida sat in the darkness, watching the orange LCD readings on the monitors and trying to focus on the rise and fall of Jason's chest.

The Blackhawk raced just above the rooftops of Baghdad, rising suddenly to avoid power lines, then dropping again to stay out of the way of any insurgent fire from the ground. After about twenty-five minutes it landed at the huge U.S. air base and supply depot in Balad, north of Baghdad. The helicopter landed on the runway and, in the wee hours of Sunday, April 18, an Air Force crew carried Jason's stretcher out of the helicopter and up the rear ramp of a four-engine C-141 transport jet bound for Germany.

———

At that moment, the wounded Iraqi known in al Qa'im as POW #1 lay just a few blocks away in the Balad branch of the 31st CSH. Back on April 14, he had shared a night medevac from al Asad to Balad with Lance Corporal Falah, who had finally stopped singing the Marine Corps Hymn and proclaiming his love for the battalion commander. The 31st CSH in Balad consisted of a maze of green sixty-four-by-twenty-two-foot tents, linked together by tunnels. The base was the frequent target of mortar and rocket attacks. Most were wildly inaccurate, but one landed just outside the crowded base store, killing two soldiers. Patients in the hospital frequently had to take cover under their cots when the loudspeakers outside bellowed, "Alarm Red. Alarm Red."

Major Malcolm Napier, an internist from Hattiesburg, Mississippi, was on duty when POW #1 was carried into the emergency ward. The Balad CSH kept its own running total of prisoners, so the staff rechristened POW #1 as Enemy Prisoner of War #549. In military parlance, only Americans and their allies were officially called POWs. Iraqis were EPWs. Dr. Napier suspected that EPW #549 was still bleeding inside, and on April 15 the surgeons opened him up again and found that the shock from one of the Marine bullets had fractured his liver and caused hemorrhaging in the back of his abdominal cavity. They replaced the sponges that Dr. Villaflor had packed around the man's liver in al Asad. On April 17, they operated again to see if the situation had changed. This time they found the bleeding had stopped and the liver was already healing. On April 18, the doctors removed the chest tube, since the hole in the Iraqi's lung had healed as well. The next day they removed the drain from his chest, and on April 20 the Iraqi was able to walk around with the aid of a physical therapist. On April 22, eight days after he was shot in Husaybah, the medical staff handed EPW #549 over to custody of the Eighty-first Detention Facility.

The Eighty-first was a collection of a few air-conditioned tents surrounded by coils of razor wire just behind the hospital. The prisoners were held there and given any necessary medical attention until they were well enough to be sent to Abu Ghraib or some other coalition prison. The security guards from the Washington State Army National Guard jokingly called it Area 51, after the facility where conspiracy theorists believed the government concealed captured space aliens. EPW #549 was one of the first to be sent to the detention center, and he and his fellow prisoners spent their days recuperating on Army cots under white sheets and baby-blue hospital blankets. At mealtimes they'd get the same military chow their guards ate, washed down with cans of Pepsi or Sprite. A bowl of fresh fruit was within reach on the table at the far end of the tent, as was a cooler full of plastic water bottles. The prisoners cleaned their own tent and helped each other walk to the latrine. They'd eat, rest, and pray to Allah. Those who could, kneeled. Those who couldn't, prayed in plastic patio chairs. Sometimes they'd sit outside when shadows appeared and the desert cooled in the evenings.

IX | *Phone Call*

Scio, New York

WHEN A MARINE from Third Battalion was killed or wounded in Iraq, commanders shut down e-mail traffic from the bases in al Qa'im and Husaybah and locked up the satellite phones to make sure that first word of the casualty did not reach his wife and parents via the Marine family grapevine. If the man was dead, his next of kin got a knock on the door and the grim sight of two uniformed Marines, a Navy chaplain, and a Navy corpsman on the stoop. If the Marine was wounded, First Lieutenant Carlos Huerta was usually the one who had to pick up the phone and deliver the news. Huerta, a twenty-seven-year-old from Tucson, had planned to leave the Marine Corps in December 2003, but, at his commanders' request, he extended his service to handle administrative matters in Twentynine Palms while the others shipped out to Iraq. He was in charge of the men who for one reason or another couldn't go to war, and of those who came home early to put their bodies and lives back together.

But the task that left Carlos bitter about the military was having to call the next of kin of the wounded men. The

Corps hadn't trained him to deal with the surprise, grief, anger, and terror that seized the men's families when they heard an unfamiliar Marine officer on the other end of the line. Several next of kin had accused the lieutenant of being an impostor playing a cruel practical joke. Sometimes the family members were in such shock when they got the news that it took them two or three minutes just to write down the lieutenant's phone number. Often they'd call back an hour later to see if there was any update on their Marine's condition. Huerta knew what he said in those first moments would be branded onto a wife, father, or mother's memory forever. More than 120 times the lieutenant had to pick up the phone and make such a call. Often he couldn't find the right words when no words were right.

If the wounded man was in good enough shape, he might have been able to borrow a satellite phone and call home from the hospitals in al Asad, Balad, or Baghdad. So, after introducing himself, Lieutenant Huerta sometimes started his phone calls by asking cautiously, "Have you heard from your son?" In those cases the parents often already knew more about their son's condition than Lieutenant Huerta could discern from the vague reports emanating from the field.

The e-mail that the lieutenant received from Marine command on Thursday, April 15, was just specific enough that he knew Jason Dunham's parents would have received no reassuring call from their son. The message arrived at 7:13 p.m. California time, while at the 31st CSH in Baghdad Captain Walker was coming off the night shift and preparing to hand over Jason's care to Lieutenant Meléndez. Huerta called First Division headquarters to make sure that he was the one who was supposed to notify the Dunhams. He hoped it was someone else's job, but it wasn't. He searched fruitlessly for more details about Jason's condition on the Marines' computerized casualty tracking system. He checked the personnel file and saw that Dan Dunham, not Deb, was listed as Jason's next of kin. He sat for several long minutes steeling himself to make the call.

It was just past 11 p.m. in Scio, forty-three hours after Jason was wounded, when the phone rang in the Dunhams' house. Dan was already asleep, and Deb sat in the living room reading a romance novel. Lieutenant Huerta introduced himself. "I'm his mother," Deb said. "What has happened to my son? Is he O.K.?"

"I need to speak to his father," Huerta said.

Deb woke Dan up. "I'm calling to notify you of an injury your son received while he was in Iraq," the lieutenant said. Then he read the e-mail to Dan, line by line.

> *Report type: Initial.*
> *Casualty type: Hostile.*
> *Casualty status: Very seriously injured.*
> *Date/time of incident: April 14, 2004, 12:20 Iraqi time.*
> *Circumstances: Corporal Dunham sustained shrapnel to the head from an explosion while conducting combat operations in the Al Anbar Province. Corporal Dunham is currently being treated at the 31st Combat Support Hospital. Purple Heart is recommended.*

"This is all the information I have," the lieutenant concluded. "Do you have any questions for me?"

Carlos was surprised by the Dunhams' even-keeled response. "When do I get my next update?" Dan asked. Huerta promised to let them know as soon as any new report arrived.

"O.K.," Dan said. "If that's all the information you have, I guess we don't have any more questions. You will call us when you get more information?"

"Definitely," Huerta assured him.

Kyle had heard the phone ring and walked into his parents' room, where he overheard Deb exclaim to Dan, "Oh, my God." Dan, still on the phone, tried to calm her down so he could hear the lieutenant. Deb closed the door, but listening from outside Kyle could still catch the drift of the conversation. He was a junior firefighter at the Scio Volunteer Fire Department and knew enough about the rescue business to know that head wounds were dangerous and hard to treat. He sat quietly in the living room as Dan and Deb called Jason's grandparents and uncle, and he tried to shut out thoughts of Jason as he fell asleep.

Katie woke up when she heard her mom crying in the middle of the night. She wandered out of her bedroom and asked what was wrong. Deb said she had been having a bad dream and sent Katie back to bed. But Katie had a feeling something terrible had happened. Her mom didn't usually cry about dreams, and her dad didn't usually look so sad.

Dan called Justin before midnight and told him that Jason had been injured, but that they didn't know how badly. Justin told his fiancée, Amy, who suggested he try not to worry about it yet. "Just see what happens when your parents call back," she said.

Jason's girlfriend Sara, who was asleep at her parents' home in Michigan, thought it odd that Dan would call at such an hour, but didn't immediately suspect the reason.

They exchanged quick greetings, and then Sara asked, "What's up?"

Dan didn't want Sara to be alone when she heard the news, and he made sure her parents were home. "We just got a call," Dan said. "Jason is injured."

Sara sat up in bed in the dark, shaking. "What do you mean injured?" she asked.

Dan summarized the e-mail. "All we know is he's in critical condition." Sara's nursing instincts kicked in and she wondered whether he was awake and what his intracranial pressure readings were. "We don't know anything, Sara," Dan said.

Their calls made, Dan sat in the living room with the television remote control, the phone, a can of Skoal, and an empty soft drink can to spit the tobacco juice into. He felt sick to his stomach. "Go get some rest," he told Deb. "This could be a long time."

Deb went to bed but got no rest. She prayed quietly: "Please heal Jason. Please bring him home to me." By three in the morning she felt such pain in her gut and heart that she curled into the fetal position around a pillow and sobbed. As her fear grew, her prayer changed: "Please don't let him be in pain. Please don't let him be alone."

She and Dan clung to one piece of hopeful news, though: they hadn't gotten a knock on the door.

_____

On a normal morning, Dan was already at the factory by the time Katie rolled out of bed. When Katie woke up on Friday, Dan was still at home and she wanted to know why. He explained that Jason had been hurt and told her what little he knew about his condition. She sat in silence in an easy chair and finally asked whether her brother would be O.K. Dan said he didn't know the answer to that question.

Deb called the neighbors and asked them to be ready on a moment's notice to look after Kyle and Katie. Then she drove to the bank in nearby Wellsville and drained the family savings, $4,600, in case she and Dan had to rush to a military hospital in Germany or Bethesda, Maryland. Barb Eck, a friend who worked the bank's drive-through window, saw Deb at the teller. Barb had known Deb a long time and could tell she had been crying. "Jason has been hit," Deb told her, bursting into tears. Barb steered Deb into the bank employees' break room. "I don't know if we have to go to Germany," Deb said. "I don't know if we have to go to Maryland. Wherever Jason needs me, I'll go."

With Deb's permission, Barb put a collection can on the counter at The Store in Scio, where she had her second job. "Send the Dunhams to Germany," the sign said. The popular Texas Hot restaurant in Wellsville put out a can, too. The Elks and Lions clubs raised money, as did Dan's coworkers. The teachers at Scio Central School dipped into the dress-down fund, into which each teacher paid one dollar on Fridays in exchange for the right to wear jeans to work that day. The staff used the money for emergencies—a teacher whose house burned down, a bus driver with cancer. Friends wrote the Dunhams personal checks for $50 or $100. Envelopes arrived in the mail with $10 or $20 in cash inside and no names or return addresses on the outside. One note said, "Use this to get to your son." All told, friends, neighbors, and strangers raised more than $8,000, in addition to the macaroni, kielbasa, and other dishes they brought by the house.

Word of Jason's injury spread fast around Scio, and rumors

soon outstripped the meager information the Dunhams themselves had. Jason had lost an arm. Jason was dead. Jason has been upgraded from critical to serious. Jason was fine. Jason had been shot. Jason had been shot in Germany. Jason's buddy Jud Lambert was studying for exams at Niagara University when he got a computer message from Justin: "Jason is in critical condition. He was injured in an attack." Jud sat by himself drinking beer. As word spread, Jason's friends flocked to Scio to stand watch and keep each other company holding up the bar at the Mahogany Ridge.

Jenny Crittenden, whom Jason had almost persuaded to enlist in the Marines, heard the news from her grandparents and drove to Maurice's Clothing Store to find Heather Brisbee, who had gotten a tattoo at Jason's urging. Heather was already in tears. During Jason's Christmas visit he had called her drunk from a party at 1:30 one night, but she had been in bed and decided not to pick up the phone. "Jason's tough," Jenny assured her. "Everything is going to be all right. He'll come home." Heather trusted Jenny's judgment and felt better.

On the evening of Saturday, April 17, Lieutenant Huerta called the Dunhams to report that Jason would soon be transferred from Baghdad to Landstuhl Regional Medical Center, the Army hospital in Germany. He told Deb that Jason was still unconscious, but that his head bandage had been removed. Neither the lieutenant nor Deb knew whether that constituted good news or bad. The lieutenant was now willing to talk to Deb directly, even if Dan wasn't around. Dan spent the evening at a stock-car race in Pennsylvania; he had promised a friend who was driving that he'd lend a hand in the pits.

On Sunday the Dunhams were watching NASCAR races

on television when Lieutenant Huerta called again to let them know that Jason had arrived in Germany. Deb asked if she and Dan should fly there, but Huerta recommended against it for fear that Jason would be shipped home quickly and they'd cross paths over the Atlantic. Deb thought Huerta seemed increasingly exasperated that he wasn't getting more details from the field about Jason's condition. His answer to many questions was still, "I don't have that information."

Deb's parents, Roberta and Jerry Kinkead, drove to Scio every day that week from Ridgeway, Pennsylvania, a four-hour round-trip. Jerry was a bluff, silver-haired man who had retired as a phone company lineman. Roberta, a reed of a woman with short hair, had worked for years at a powdered metal factory. The Kinkeads used to sneak Jason a few dollars behind Deb and Dan's backs when he found himself short for a cross-country drive or some other venture. With each passing day, Roberta, in particular, grew more incensed that the military wasn't providing detailed information about Jason's injury and prospects for recovery. The gnawing uncertainty reminded Dan's mother, Pat Layton, of the Vietnam War, when her family waited in anguish for two weeks to learn whether her brother had survived a devastating attack on the Army base where he was stationed. Pat knew the military moved slowly at times, but the news about Jason was so sparse that she felt like screaming.

Deb was frustrated, too, and dazed with worry and exhaustion after several nearly sleepless nights. But she kept telling herself that Jason would be fine in the end, and the last thing she wanted was to get him in trouble with the Marine Corps by being too much of a pest. She also worried that complaining might alienate someone who could otherwise provide her with information about Jason down the road.

Another day passed without news, however, and on Tuesday, April 20, six days after Jason was wounded, Deb's desperation overwhelmed her caution.

While Dan took the trash to the dump and visited the factory to thank his colleagues for their kindness, Deb called the Wellsville office of the American Red Cross and asked for help. The representative contacted the Dunhams' congressman, Amo Houghton, who had been a Marine private first class during World War II. When the Marine Corps commandant, General Michael Hagee, visited the House of Representatives each November to host a reception for the Corps' birthday, it fell by tradition to the youngest former Marine and oldest former Marine in Congress to share a piece of birthday cake. The youngest was a representative from Illinois who served during the Vietnam War. Houghton, at seventy-seven, was the oldest, and it gave him a special relationship with the commandant. Deb knew none of that, but she was glad to have any help she could get. Still, she worried about the reaction from the Marines, and she immediately called Lieutenant Huerta to apologize for going over his head. He apologized for not having been able to get her more news about Jason. "You've got to do what you've got to do," he said.

Soon Congressman Houghton's aide called and asked Deb's leave to intervene. Lieutenant Huerta called back to tell Deb that he had just found out Jason would arrive at Andrews Air Force Base, outside Washington, D.C., the next night and would be taken to the National Naval Medical Center in Bethesda, Maryland. Deb assumed she and Dan should stay at Andrews to be close to Jason. She called the base and stumbled upon a kind Air Force staff sergeant who agreed to sponsor them to stay in base lodging, usually off-limits to civilians. Katie and a family friend began packing food in a cooler for the car trip Deb thought they'd be making to Washington.

Early that morning Deb had received a call from a Buffalo television reporter, who passed along an e-mail the station had received from Brad Cress, a Marine staff sergeant from the area. At the time, Staff Sergeant Cress had been temporarily assigned to play the role of a Marine drill instructor in a military stage show honoring the new World War II memorial on the National Mall. The acting job was a constant reminder of how far he was from the men fighting in Iraq. So when he ran across a story about Jason Dunham's injury on the television station's Web site, he wrote the station offering his assistance. At first Deb had thought the offer kind, but unnecessary. By afternoon, however, she was willing to call a complete stranger for help. Cress put her in touch with Staff Sergeant Miguel Cruz at Bethesda. "Ma'am," Cruz asked, "what is going on?" She told her story. Cruz explained that she couldn't stay at Andrews Air Force Base; during rush hour it could take her an hour to get around the Beltway to the hospital to see her son.

"Honey, there's one red light in this town," Deb said. "I have no concept what you're talking about." Deb told Cruz that she and Dan planned to drive to Maryland the next day. Cruz thought that upset as Deb clearly was, it was unwise for her and Dan to be on the road for six hours. Less than twenty minutes later Cruz called back to tell Deb that she and Dan had tickets waiting for them to fly from Rochester to Washington the next morning. He promised lodging and a Marine reception at the airport. "Your mother raised you well," Deb told him.

"Things could be the other way around," Cruz responded. "It could be me arriving here, and I would expect my fellow Marines to treat my family the same way I would treat yours."

Dan came home that afternoon with a Post-it note from a guy at work whose wife worked for the Red Cross. "I have phone numbers," he said.

"I have tickets," Deb answered.

"You did better," Dan said.

That evening Deb obsessed over the long list of things she felt she had to get done before she could go to Bethesda. She had to pay bills. She had to pack her bags. She had to type out a permission slip so that a friend could authorize medical care for Katie and Kyle in case something happened to them. She had to arrange for Wrexie Ames, the next-door neighbor, to stay with the kids. She had to get the laundry done. Deb went into her sewing room and ironed frenetically, on the verge of tears.

"I can do your ironing," Wrexie offered.

"But they're our clothes," Deb insisted, unable to accept that someone else would do her work for her.

"I know how to iron," Wrexie said gently, and she picked up the iron.

Deb packed the first Harry Potter novel in her suitcase. She figured Jason was in for a long recovery, and she wanted to have something to read aloud at his bedside when she and Dan ran out of things to say.

x | *Civilization*

Landstuhl, Germany

IF YOU MAKE it to Landstuhl, you're good to go.

It was an article of faith among the Marine infantrymen in Iraq that if the corpsman plugged up the hole to keep you from bleeding out, and the field surgeons stitched up the important organs, and the Air Force got you all the way to the Army hospital in Landstuhl, Germany, then you'd live. You might not be the same. Your legs might not be where they were before the war. Your arms might not work as well. Your skin might be disfigured by burns. Your brain might be so badly injured that you might not really be the same person you used to be. But you'd survive and eventually get home to your parents, your wife, your kids, your girl.

The tidy town of Landstuhl lay snug in a valley in southwestern Germany, surrounded by hills covered with birch, mountain maple, and black locust. It was dominated by the bustling Landstuhl Regional Medical Center and the 40,000 Americans who lived in the area. The commissaries and PX stores at Landstuhl and Ramstein Air Base, in nearby Kaiserslautern, carried food, electronics, and clothes familiar to homesick Americans. American military expats traveled there from as far away as Belgium to do their shopping, and Kaiserslautern happily billed itself as the American City in Europe. Every U.S. Marine, soldier, sailor, and airman wounded badly enough in Iraq or Afghanistan to be sent home passed through this corner of Germany.

———

It had been the middle of the night back in Eureka, California, when Pfc. Kelly Miller was wounded by the hand grenade in the H-K Triangle. A few hours later his mother Linda had sat up in bed in a panic, sure something terrible had happened to her son. That afternoon, she got the news that confirmed her premonition when Kelly borrowed a satellite phone from a cute nurse at Balad air base. Charlie answered. "Hi, Dad," Kelly said. "Where's Mom?" Linda was out getting her nails done. "I was involved in an incident in Iraq, and I'm on my way to Germany," Kelly told Charlie.

Charlie drove to the beauty shop to find Linda and told her that Kelly had called. Linda thought that odd. "That's nice. What did he have to say?"

Charlie was silent for a long moment. "Kelly has been hurt, and they're flying him to Germany."

"How bad?"

"I don't know," Charlie admitted. "I didn't ask."

Pfc. Miller's medevac flight left Balad air base early on April 15, fifteen hours after he was hit in the H-K Triangle. Kelly passed out during the four-hour flight, but was awake as the medics at Ramstein were loading his stretcher into an olive drab Army school bus. On the way to Landstuhl, he gazed out the window at the green hills, wet and foggy. The sight was a shock after months in the desert and reminded him of

Eureka. When he arrived in the ward, the nurses changed his bandages. The wound in Miller's right triceps went clean through, and a male nurse ran a long swab through the hole. It didn't hurt as much as Kelly expected, and he thought it looked cool to have a pierced arm. He gave the nurse ten dollars to go to the gift shop and buy a disposable camera. Kelly posed with a toothy grin, a red-stained gauze bandage dangling out of the hole in his arm. "Dude—that's my Christmas card right there," he told the nurse. The other arm wasn't so funny. It was tight from swelling, and the gauze packed into the wounds had dried and stuck to the flesh. He asked for more morphine as the nurses tore the bandages away. Later the doctors took him into surgery to clean out the wounds.

Afterward, Kelly called his mother. "So, Kelly," Linda said. "I have to ask—did you lose any body parts?"

"No, Mom."

"So what are your injuries?"

Kelly said he had been hit by shrapnel in the arms and face. "My fucking arm looks like I have elephantiasis."

"If I could get over there would you like me to come?" Linda asked.

"That would be nice," Kelly said.

Linda swung into action. She called a retired colonel who had run a U.S. air base in Germany and asked whether he could help get her on a flight. She called Lieutenant Huerta at Twentynine Palms, who suggested that Kelly probably wouldn't be in Germany long enough to make the trip worthwhile for her. At Kelly's request, Linda tracked down a nurse at Landstuhl and tried to find out how Jason was doing. Linda discovered that the Marine Corps posted liaisons at every major hospital to ensure that the wounded and their families were surrounded by other Marines and got whatever nonmedical assistance they needed. She called the liaison office at Landstuhl and talked to a sergeant. "Your son is doing well," he assured her. "He's injured, but not seriously injured."

Miller traded war stories with his new roommate, Corporal Thompson, the Marine from the sniper team who had been shot through both legs near the Crackhouse. Thompson alternated between complaining about the pain and apologizing to the nurses for complaining about the pain. By autumn, he had undergone seven operations on his legs. At one point a retired Army officer stopped by to talk, and Kelly lamented that he had turned twenty-one years old twelve days before getting hit and still hadn't had his first legal beer. The soldier came back with cold bottles of German beer for Miller and Thompson, pouring them into cups to fool the nurses. A chaplain visited and was struck by Miller's compulsion to talk about the incident in the H-K Triangle. The chaplain put a note in Kelly's record: *Post-traumatic stress disorder follow-up will be needed.*

Many of the wounded arrived in Germany naked, their clothes cut off their backs by corpsmen in the field or elsewhere along the way. The Marine liaisons provided each injured man with a $250 voucher to spend at the Landstuhl PX. Miller went shopping with Lance Corporal Falah, Lieutenant Colonel Lopez's bodyguard. Miller splurged on Nike gear—shorts, warm-ups, cross-trainers. Falah shopped in a wheelchair.

Falah had been in a morphine cloud when he arrived at the hospital at Balad air base the night of April 14. He came to and found himself in a tent full of wounded Iraqis.

"Oorah!" he shouted at them. "Look at you. You're whining like a bunch of little bitches." In mid-diatribe, Falah realized something was wrong; he was the only patient in the tent who wasn't Iraqi. Where were his buddies? Falah wondered. Where were the guys he got hurt with? Then the morphine pushed him back into unconsciousness.

Falah wasn't sure how much time passed before an Army doctor woke him up and asked in rudimentary Arabic if he was in pain. "*Alam? Alam?*" the doctor said. It suddenly hit Falah that the man thought he was an Iraqi prisoner.

"What the fuck are you talking about?" Falah asked.

"You speak English?" the surprised doctor replied.

"I'm a fucking Marine," Falah said angrily.

"Oh, I'm sorry," the doctor said. The doctors moved him to one of the tents for injured Americans.

Falah borrowed a satellite telephone and called Nancy Leigh, the assistant manager of the building where his father lived. Falah hadn't seen his own mother in close to fifteen years, and relations with his father, Walid, were strained. Nancy had become Akram's surrogate mother. "Ma, we got in a gun battle, and I got shot," Falah told her. Then he called Walid, a cashier at a California gas station. Walid hadn't been surprised when Akram joined the Marines. His son had always been fascinated with the military and could converse knowledgeably about battles in World War I and World War II. Besides, Walid thought it was a good way to repay the United States for welcoming them. Now he suspected that Falah didn't want to scare him by revealing how bad the injury really was.

"How is it?" Walid said. "Tell me the truth."

"I don't know right now," Falah said.

Each bump in the road between Ramstein Air Base and

Landstuhl sent a spike of pain into Falah's arm, and he screamed much of the way. The first time he got a good look at his own wound was when the nurses changed his dressing. He saw fat, muscle, and bone, and feared he was going to lose the arm. It suddenly dawned on him that he might not be able to go back to Iraq. He decided it would be his fault if something happened to Lieutenant Colonel Lopez. One night another wounded Marine yelled "Mortars!" in his sleep. Falah dove underneath his own cot and screamed, "In Germany, too?"

Falah took comfort in the proximity of Miller and Thompson, however. Long after he left Germany, Falah remembered holding Thompson's hand and urging him to be strong. Thompson, in a painkiller haze, didn't remember that Falah had been in Landstuhl at all. His memories came back slowly as a fuzzy slide show: A couple of plane rides. Having hiccups for two days. A nurse who worried because Thompson looked like he was shooting people in his sleep. Dreaming that he was Spiderman.

Lance Corporal Hampton had woken up after dark on April 14 when the helicopter from the shock-trauma tent in al Qa'im landed at Alpha Surgical Company in al Asad. He soon found himself sharing a room with several of the other Third Battalion Marines hit that day: Corporal Lightfoot, Lance Corporal Whittenberg, Lance Corporal Roshak, Captain Lewis, and Pfc. Simental. Most of the men hadn't known each other before, but they clung together, sharing the pain of their wounds and the relief at having survived the day. They held each other's IV bags when they went to the bathroom and swapped stories about how they had been wounded. They made up nicknames for each other: Hampton was Pepper because his arms and legs were dotted with shrapnel wounds. Lightfoot was Sprinkler because of the noise he made when he hopped down the hall in his flip-flops to have a cigarette. Whittenberg was Ass Man or Forrest Gump for his wounded rear end. Roshak was inevitably dubbed Splinter. Lewis was an officer and got no nickname.

The surgeons removed Roshak's wooden spike; it turned out that it hadn't gone in very deep and had missed the artery. He was soon back on duty. The doctors promised to save the splinter for him, but it got lost in the shuffle and Roshak never saw it. At home six months later he got a copy of the digital photo the corpsman had taken of him in al Qa'im. He and his buddies immediately installed it on their cell phones for decoration. Lightfoot watched with detachment as doctors operated on his foot with a local anesthetic, but he found it excruciating later on when he had to pack and unpack his own gauze bandages, which inevitably stuck to the open wound. Hampton serenaded Whittenberg with country music while the nurses repacked gauze in the hole in his rear end.

Whittenberg borrowed a guitar from one of the nurses and played songs by REM, Nirvana, and others, including one about the boys from Oklahoma rolling their joints all wrong, "way too skinny, way too long." Someone bought them Cokes, candy bars, and *Maxim* magazines from the PX. Hampton told Lightfoot what had happened on the narrow lane in the H-K Triangle, and they discussed under what circumstances they'd be willing to jump on a hand grenade.

Captain Lewis, the battalion lawyer, made sure everyone got to make a satellite phone call home. Early in the morning on Friday, April 16, blood suddenly gushed out of the drainage tube the surgeons had inserted in the captain's wounded left arm. The bullet had nicked the brachial artery, and the slow seepage that had been swelling his arm became a torrent onto the bedsheets. The doctors calculated that he had lost several pints of blood. In the middle of a cool night a helicopter carried him to the Green Zone and then to Balad. The doctors there were fascinated by the idea of a wounded attorney, and he received many visits from unfamiliar officers. Surgeons repaired the artery and made an incision from his biceps to his wrist and cut open the fascia, the thin tissue covering the muscle, to relieve the pressure inside his arm. It took almost two months for the wound to close.

At al Asad Hampton heard about Corporal Dunham's escape from the expectant ward and thought it was just like Dunham to pull off a miracle recovery. When Bill moved to the 31st CSH in Baghdad, however, he found the reality less reassuring. He limped up the hospital stairs and along the hall to the ICU, glancing as he passed at the wounded Iraqi prisoners in their beds. He stood at Jason's side, shocked by the damage the grenade had done to his face. He touched Jason's arm and stared at an Iraqi patient in the next bed, whose hands were frozen in clawlike anguish. Bill tried talking to Jason a bit. "Hey, bud, it's me, Hampton." He tried to sound comforting and assured Jason that everything would turn out fine. But the sight of his squad leader's bandaged head brought back memories of a guy named Tony he had known in high school, who had died slowly of a head injury from a car accident. Bill felt himself on the verge of breaking down and didn't trust himself to speak. He stood next to Jason in silence and after a few minutes returned glumly to his own cot.

The doctors scheduled both Hampton and Dunham for the April 18 early morning medevac from Balad air base to Germany, and Bill was already on board when the Air Force crew brought Jason's stretcher off the helicopter from Baghdad and up the rear ramp of the plane. The slender, battleship-gray jet, a relic from the Vietnam era, had flown in from Germany filled with war cargo, and in less than an hour the Air Force medical team had turned the empty cargo bay into a flying hospital, stacking stretchers four high on stanchions down the center of the fuselage and running oxygen lines down the sides.

The Air Force crew loaded the walking wounded first, followed by the stretcher cases and finally the men in critical condition. In part the intention was to spare the worst-off a long wait on the plane. But the thinking also reflected the rigors of military triage. If the base came under attack during the loading and the pilot had to take off to escape damage, it was better from a military point of view to depart with the patients the doctors knew they could save and leave behind the ones who might die anyway. The critical patients, however, received special medical attention and had teams of ICU specialists devoted to their care on the flight. Sometimes the nurses stood strapped to their patients' stretchers in case the wounded men reacted badly to the swerving maneuvers the pilots conducted to avoid antiaircraft fire as they left Iraq. The crews flew with the lights off for the first forty-five minutes or so to make sure they were invisible from the ground, and the medical teams watched their charges with red or blue headlamps or flashlights until the lights came on in the cargo bay.

Lightfoot, Simental, and Whittenberg lay on litters. Hampton couldn't even make a fist with his left hand and had to rely on a nurse to hold a cup for him when he urinated. A pediatric anesthesiologist on detail from a Texas air base was assigned to care for Jason during the flight, and he was alarmed by the periodic pressure spikes inside Jason's skull. As the plane maneuvered after takeoff, the numbers rose from the midteens to the midtwenties, a dangerous level. Jason coughed and the reading went up again. The doctor elevated Jason's head and gave him more mannitol, the same drug that Steve Noakes had administered in al Asad and the CSH nurses had given him in Baghdad. The doctor also increased the dose of sedatives, hoping the combination would relieve the pressure.

Jason's ambulance raced ahead of the bus carrying the other wounded men from Ramstein Air Base to Landstuhl, where gurneys and attendants were lined up waiting at the hospital entrance like runners at the starting line. The ambulance pulled into the circular drive at 10 a.m. on April 18, and Sergeant Justin McConnell from the Marine liaison office was there to greet it. The twenty-five-year-old Sergeant McConnell had been studying nuclear engineering and business management at the University of Missouri in tiny Rolla when he was called up from the Reserve and sent to Landstuhl. Pfc. Miller had told the sergeant what had happened in the H-K Triangle, and he knew from the advisory sent from Baghdad that Corporal Dunham was arriving in critical condition. He held Jason's hand as he walked alongside the gurney on the way up to the intensive care unit. "I'm Sergeant McConnell with the Marine liaisons here," he said. "You're in Landstuhl, Germany. We're here to take care of you."

The ICU rooms were stripped to the bare essentials: an adjustable bed with white and green sheets, a tall metal rack loaded with monitoring equipment, a beige linoleum floor, and pinkish curtains to keep the sun out. Sergeant McConnell watched as the Air Force doctor handed Jason over to the Army medical team led by Colonel Bernard Roth, a pulmonary critical care specialist. When the nurses pushed his gurney into Room 5, Jason's pressure reading was less than 10.

It took seven people to move Jason onto the bed, three on each side and one holding his head. As soon as they lifted him off the gurney, his intracranial pressure reading shot up to 32. The ICU always kept mannitol on hand, but sometimes the sugary drug crystallized in its storage vials and couldn't be used until it had been held under warm water long enough for the crystals to dissolve. As an urgent measure Dr. Roth ordered First Lieutenant Richard Ferrell, the ICU nurse, to turn up the pace of Jason's ventilator to twenty breaths per minute. Hyperventilation expels carbon dioxide from the system, and removing carbon dioxide leads the blood vessels in the brain to constrict. It wasn't a long-term solution, but rather a quick fix to get Jason past a moment of crisis until the mannitol was ready.

Lieutenant Ferrell had been working in the ICU at Bakersfield Memorial Hospital in California when his Army Reserve unit was called up. The Bakersfield hospital had no trauma ward, and he mostly dealt with seventy- and eighty-year-olds there who had suffered strokes or heart attacks or contracted other ailments of the tail end of life. He had once worked in a trauma ward in Colorado and thought that his experience there with injured gang members and bystanders would prepare him to care for battle casualties. When he got to Germany he quickly realized he was wrong: the injuries were far more ghastly, the injured far younger, the work far more depressing.

Ferrell wasn't surprised to see Jason's intracranial pressure rise; he had seen enough head wounds by then to know they left patients susceptible to pressure fluctuations when they coughed or vomited or just changed positions. But he was surprised by how far and fast the reading jumped. Within ten minutes, however, the combination of hyperventilation and then warmed-up mannitol reduced the pressure in Jason's head to an acceptable level, to the great relief of the ICU team. Dr. Roth immediately ordered Jason taken to radiology for new CT scans to see if his pressure spike reflected some turn for the worse inside his head. The doctor suspected the cause was a faulty monitor, and he called Baghdad to get the code necessary to recalibrate the machine. After he entered the new code, Jason's readings dropped below 10.

During Jason's first few minutes in the ward, Lieutenant Ferrell inspected him from head to toe. The lieutenant knew Jason had already been through several hospitals in Iraq, but it was standard practice to act as if he were the first nurse to see each ICU patient. A top killer of trauma patients was an injury missed that could otherwise have been treated, and the Landstuhl medical team knew virtually nothing about what had happened to Corporal Dunham on a distant battlefield. Some hospital records had him listed as a private first class. Some said he had been injured in an ambush by an improvised explosive device, a roadside bomb. The Marine patient-tracking system reported that he had been hit by a mortar. Other records said GSW—gunshot wound. Sometimes he was identified as Jason Durham. On one form Dr. Roth's resident just noted that Jason had an "explosion injury to the head." He checked the box for "Very seriously ill" and under prognosis had a choice between "Recovery is not expected" and "Questionable." He chose "Questionable."

Jason was hooked up to a plethora of medical equipment over the course of the day: There was the intracranial pressure monitor. There was a catheter that passed through his urethra to drain his bladder into a bag. A line ran into his left femoral artery to monitor his blood pressure and allow the nurses to draw blood samples easily. He had a rectal temperature probe. On the right side of his groin was a triple-headed catheter running into a vein for IV fluids and drugs. There was an endotracheal tube in his mouth to facilitate passage of air between the ventilator and his lungs, plus a suction tube to draw excess fluid from his lungs and an oral gastric tube to suck out stomach acid. Compression sleeves on both calves alternately squeezed and relaxed to keep blood moving through his legs and prevent clots. Five pads on his chest monitored his heart rate. A blood oxygen monitor was clipped onto his finger. A manual blood pressure cuff was on his arm in case the automatic reading failed. The nurses put a sterile plastic cup under each ear to collect the cerebrospinal fluid that continued to drain through his burst eardrums.

The doctors also kept Jason on a pharmacopoeia of drugs. They gave him two heavy-duty antibiotics to fight off infection, including vancomycin, one of the most powerful bacteria killers known. He was on Dilantin to prevent seizures that might be induced by jumps in intracranial pressure, and on mannitol to control the pressure itself. He was on two drugs to keep him calm and painless: Propofol, a sedative called milk of amnesia for its erasing effect on short-term memories; and fentanyl, a painkilling narcotic so powerful that it makes morphine seem like children's aspirin by comparison. Without them his blood pressure and intracranial pressure both rose sharply. He was on Tylenol to keep his fever in check, and Zantac because stress can cause adrenalin buildups, which can lead to ulcers.

The ICU nurses especially liked dealing with Marines.

The grunts rarely griped, and if they did, all the nurses had to do was address them sternly as "Marine" in order to shut them up. One ICU nurse once prepped a Marine for an arm amputation. The man lay in bed bemoaning his fate until the nurse asked him to describe his specialty in the Marine Corps. The Marine spent the next twenty minutes describing his machine gun in loving detail, and six hours after the surgery asked for a prosthetic arm so he could ride his dirt bike and play video games. Lieutenant Ferrell treated a Marine patient on a ventilator who used hand signals to indicate he wanted to be sent back to his unit at the front.

The nurses were also impressed that the Marine Corps, alone among the services, had set up a liaison office in the hospital to take care of its fallen. That evening Sergeant McConnell and a chaplain's assistant went up to Jason's room before going home. They told him about Miller and Hampton. "They're doing all right," the sergeant said. "They want to come up and see you. We're not sure if they can do that."

Over the next couple of days, Bill Hampton managed to talk his way into Jason's room. "Hey, dude," Bill said, looking out the window at the greenery. "You should wake up and check out this view." He tried to make conversation, but found being with Jason overwhelming.

Bill's stay in Germany struck him as absurdly disconnected from the life he had just left behind in Iraq. Hampton's roommate at the hospital, an Air Force enlisted man, was curious about Bill's injuries. Hampton explained that he'd been hit by hand grenade fragments. "What happened to you?" he asked the airman. The man's chin dropped to his chest as he mumbled, "I've got a rash on my foot." Hampton was too stunned to laugh. He just walked out, went to the Landstuhl enlisted men's club with Corporal Lightfoot, and drank a

Heineken. One evening Hampton, Lightfoot, and Simental went to the town of Kaiserslautern, ate a veal dinner at a German restaurant, and found their way to an Irish pub. Lance Corporal Whittenberg was already there doing shots. They flirted with the bartender and drank tiny cups of potent Austrian butterscotch rum and mugs of warm Guinness. They stumbled into a taxi, and Whittenberg passed out on the way back to the hospital. Hampton's arm was in a sling, and both Lightfoot and Simental were on crutches, so they couldn't carry Whittenberg inside.

Whittenberg remained in Germany for three weeks while the doctors made sure his wound didn't get infected. His parents flew over to visit him. Then he returned to the combat zone.

The CT scans taken the day Corporal Dunham arrived in Germany gave Dr. Roth little reason to believe that he was improving with time; the swelling inside his skull hadn't subsided and appeared to signal deep and lasting damage. But Dr. Roth wanted to see if Jason's brain functions were really as severely impaired as the scans suggested they were, so on the morning of Monday, April 19, he ordered the nurses to reduce the flow of sedatives through the IV. The sedatives inhibited neurological responses even in healthy patients, so he had no choice but to cut back on the drugs to see if Jason was as unresponsive as he appeared. Dr. Roth pinched the skin on Jason's clavicle, prompting Jason to posture both by pushing his hands down and away and by curling them up to his chest. Jason just coughed and shrugged his shoulders when the doctors moved his ventilator tube. He neither reacted to verbal commands, nor showed other signs of conscious response. Dr. Roth gave him a Glasgow coma score of 4, a foreboding grade.

Dr. Roth didn't question Dr. Gullick and Dr. Poffenbarger's decision to operate on Jason in Baghdad. But he believed that in the heat of battle, the neurosurgeons in the field
had gotten swept up by an unjustified sense of optimism, despite the severity of Jason's wounds. Gullick and Poffenbarger
looked on the bright side for every patient who came in the
door; Roth felt it was his job to take a step back and consider
whether Jason's life would be worth saving if he were forever
in a vegetative state in a nursing home. If Jason were showing
signs of improvement, that would be one thing. But Jason's
CT scans were as dismal as they had been when he had arrived in Baghdad from the expectant ward, and his neurological symptoms were just as bad, if not worse. Dr. Roth began
to plan not for Jason's recovery, but for his final trip home.

On April 20 he ordered another CT scan and another
neurological exam, hoping he might prove his fears un-
founded. The day's tests, however, revealed no change in Jason's condition, except that he had contracted a case of
aspiration pneumonia and that the Iraqi bacteria, *Acinetobacter
baumannii*, had crept into his system. It was, Dr. Roth noted
in Jason's record that day, a "poor prognosis injury."

Nonetheless, the ICU nurses joked with Jason as if he
were already awake. While giving Jason a bath that morning,
one nurse told him a favorite. "Two cannibals are sitting
down eating a clown. One cannibal says to the other, 'Does
this taste funny to you?' " The nurses wanted to believe
things would work out, and they saw enough amazing recoveries to remain believers.

But just in case, the ICU staff called the Marine liaisons
and suggested they make sure the Naval hospital in Bethesda
had a chaplain available for Corporal Dunham's parents.

XI | *Life Support*

Bethesda, Maryland

WHEN DEB AND Dan Dunham arrived at the National Naval Medical Center on the morning of Wednesday, April 21, they expected a military base. They found instead an extensive campus of manicured lawns and pine trees on Wisconsin Avenue, a busy commercial street that runs from the pricey suburb of Bethesda through Washington, D.C., and ends in elegant Georgetown. Despite the hospital's distance from the sea, the sign above the main entrance reads "Welcome Aboard" in the Navy fashion. Dominating the lobby is a wooden sculpture of a Navy corpsman pulling a wounded Marine out of harm's way. The Marine hangs limp in the doc's arms, his feet dragging and his arms loose. The sculpture is titled *The Unspoken Bond*, for the tie between the grunts and the sailors who tend to their wounds.

Jason wasn't due to arrive from Germany until late in the evening, and Deb and Dan were hungry for any information they could get about his condition. One of the Marine liaisons read through a manila file folder and told the Dunhams that Jason was unconscious and that his left pupil was blown.

Deb didn't know the term meant Jason's pupil was dilated and didn't react to light; she thought it meant he was missing an eye. She consoled herself with thoughts of the Dunhams' one-eyed dog Ernie, who got on well enough. "Is he on life support?" Deb asked.

The Marine could tell from the file that Jason was in very bad shape. But he was an administrator, not a doctor, and he didn't want to say anything definitive about Jason's condition. "He is on a ventilator," he told Deb.

The Marines installed Deb and Dan at the Fisher House, a pair of colonial-style brick homes on the base where families can stay while their loved ones go through treatment. During peacetime, the fifteen rooms were usually filled with the spouses and relatives of cancer patients and others entitled to military health care. The war had changed that, and the Fisher House was now crowded with families waiting for their wounded Marines and sailors to recover. The families shared a kitchen and cleaned their own rooms. They barbecued together on the flagstone patio, where big Asian goldfish dodged visiting herons. Mostly they consoled each other and swapped tips for getting through the turmoil they all faced.

The Dunhams went up to the room for a restless nap just before 1 p.m. The hours crept by, and Deb and Dan looked for ways to hurry them along. They walked to the base McDonald's for salads and browsed at the Navy Exchange store. Dan bought a pair of sneakers to walk in, even though they seemed expensive. Deb bought a notebook; one of the fathers at the Fisher House had warned that the medical information could get confusing and suggested she keep a record. Deb was also worried that they'd spend too much money, so she started keeping track of where every penny went: $29.61

for Cheerios, tea, milk, peanut butter, bread, and other groceries, $50 for Dan's sneakers, and $15.50 for breakfast at the
International House of Pancakes.

Lance Corporal Chris Trusler from the Marine liaison office picked up Deb and Dan at 9 p.m. and escorted them to
the waiting room outside the intensive care unit. He thought
the Dunhams seemed in good spirits under the circumstances. Trusler, a twenty-four-year-old from Pensacola, had
left the Corps more than three years earlier and had been
making good money installing security systems when he got
called back to active duty. For the past three weeks he had
been living at a hotel two minutes from the medical center,
his life revolving around injured men and their families. It
was emotionally draining duty. At one point that spring
Trusler sat with a Navy Seabee paralyzed by mortar fragments. The man could communicate only by blinking in
code. The message he sent his doctors was "Kill me." But
Trusler found it a relief to be back within the Marine brotherhood, and serving as a hospital liaison made him consider
reenlisting.

Trusler's commander, thirty-nine-year-old Lieutenant
Colonel Jim Byrne, was working as a federal prosecutor, going after Colombian drug traffickers, when he volunteered
for active duty. He expected to end up at the Naval base in
Guantánamo Bay, Cuba, prosecuting Taliban and al Qaeda
suspects. Instead, the Marines sent him to Bethesda to head
the liaison unit. Byrne drove to Andrews Air Force Base
Wednesday night to meet the plane from Germany and
watched the crew load Corporal Dunham's litter into a private ambulance waiting on the tarmac. The colonel sat for a
few minutes next to Jason. The noise from the plane was
deafening, and Byrne leaned over to speak into his ear: "Wel-

come back, hero. We're going to take care of you." It was the colonel's standard greeting for a wounded man. Byrne had no idea if Jason could hear him, but just in case he explained that they were at the air base where the president's plane landed, and that he was going to be taken to the Naval hospital in Bethesda.

The ambulance swung around the Capital Beltway and down Wisconsin Avenue, its siren wailing. It pulled in beneath the overhang at the emergency entrance, next to the decontamination station built for casualties of chemical or biological attacks. Attendants lifted Jason's green stretcher onto a gurney and rolled him feet first into the elevator and up to a beige ICU room with brown trim and a picture window looking onto the ward.

––––––

Command Master Chief Jim Piner, a compact man with more than twenty-three years in the Navy under his belt, was the senior enlisted adviser to the admiral in command of the hospital. At least that was his day job. Informally, Jim and his wife Sarah, a former Army intelligence analyst he met in Bosnia, were crisis counselors for the hundreds of distraught wives, husbands, fathers, and mothers who passed through Bethesda, people often from humble backgrounds whose lives had in an instant been turned inside out. The Piners lived fifty feet from the back of the Fisher House, and they always left their home open to the confused, aching families who came and went. The result was an around-the-clock parade of grief to their doorstep, ending in amazing recoveries and tragic suffering. The Piners provided a sympathetic ear and an escort through the military bureaucracy. The Piners' toddlers, Bailey and Paul, were passed from lap to lap, surrogates for children too hurt to embrace. Sarah, a twenty-eight-year-old who still wore her brunette hair in the short trim of an Army sergeant, drove families to Wal-Mart or Target to pick up necessities. For a while the Piners hosted barbecues for the Fisher House families every time Jim got paid. The cost drained their account, so Jim and Sarah persuaded their church to help foot the bill.

Jim Piner and a Navy colleague took it upon themselves to visit every wounded Marine and sailor on arrival at the hospital. They'd inspect each patient and afterward sit down with the family members to prepare them for what they'd see when they went into the room. Sometimes it was gruesome: severed arms, open face wounds, missing jaws. Nonetheless, Piner found it relieved the family's angst to know in advance what their son or, more rarely, daughter would look like. On the night of April 21, it fell to Jim Piner to sit down with Dan and Deb Dunham in the ICU lounge and tell them what they were about to see. Piner and Trusler walked the Dunhams to Jason's room, where small Marine Corps and U.S. flags signaled the presence of a Marine. The nurse warned the Dunhams that Jason might have brought home the Iraqi bacteria and advised them to put on latex gloves if they planned to touch him.

Dan and Deb walked into the room and saw Jason lying naked on his back, a towel covering his groin and a catheter tube running to a urine bag by the foot of the bed. His head was wrapped in gauze, and the left side of his face was a mask of purple and red. He wore a neck brace that tilted his head slightly. Both eyes were still swollen shut, and the Dunhams imagined an empty left eye socket beneath the inflammation. His lips and tongue, which protruded next to the plastic breathing tube, looked parched. The ventilator moved his chest up and down in a perfect, robotic rhythm. His feet curled toward each other in an exaggerated pigeon-toed posture. Dan thought he looked thin, as if his muscles were already fading. Deb thought he looked cold. "I'd love to put one of those blankets on him," she said.

"I know that's instinct," the nurse responded, "but we're trying to cool him off."

Deb sat in a chair on Jason's more heavily damaged left side, and Dan sat across from her. They each held one of Jason's hands, and they held each other's hands across Jason's stomach. "We love you," Dan assured Jason. "You're going to be all right."

"Hi, honey," Deb said. "We're here. You're home, and we're here." The doctor planned to conduct tests on Jason until dawn. So around midnight Deb walked out of Jason's room to the middle of the ward, took off her surgical gloves, and washed her hands. She bent over and cried into the sink, worried that if she wept too loudly she'd wake the other patients.

As they walked back to the Fisher House, Deb worked out how they'd reshape their lives around Jason's recovery over the coming months and years. The first thing she'd do was to call Kyle and have him give the next two Harry Potter novels to his grandmother to bring to Bethesda. "We're going to go through book one pretty fast," she told Dan. Deb figured she'd have to stay in Bethesda until the next school year started in September, and then Dan might have to retire so he could care for Jason when she went back to teaching. She worried aloud that when Jason was healthy again the Marines would send him back to Iraq.

Over the years Dan had seen Jason get banged up pretty badly. He had broken an arm once and another time had gotten a welding rod stuck in his skull. But what Dan had seen tonight was something different. He saw no future when he looked at Jason's face and felt like his son was already saying good-bye. "He doesn't look too bad," Dan lied to Deb as they sat by the goldfish pond.

Sarah Piner wasn't in the mood to console anxious parents that night. But Jim wanted her to meet the Dunhams. They strolled across the parking lot to Fisher House, and Sarah was surprised to feel an instant kinship with Deb. It was a clear night, with stars visible through the lights of Bethesda. The sight cheered Sarah and made her think anything was possible. Later, the Piners' three-year-old daughter Bailey crawled into Deb's lap and said, "Mommy said I had to give you a hug because you need it and I give good hugs." Sarah went to bed planning her friendship with Deb.

The doctor on the overnight shift sent Jason for a CT scan to see if anything had changed from the images taken in Landstuhl. The black-and-white pictures showed that the injured left side of Jason's brain was pushing almost a centimeter into the right side. The metal fragment had caused enormous damage to his frontal lobe, which determined his ability to speak, and to his temporal lobe, which determined his ability to understand the speech of others. The outer surface of his brain, usually deeply grooved, instead was so puffed up that it filled his entire skull. His temporal lobe was so swollen that it was squeezing his brain stem.

Commander Jim Dunne, a trauma surgeon, arrived at the hospital in the early morning of Thursday, April 22, and looked over Jason's CT scans. At 7:30 a.m. he walked into the operating room and interrupted Lieutenant Commander

Lisa Mulligan, a neurosurgeon, in the middle of spinal surgery. "Have you seen the CT scan?" Dr. Dunne asked her. "I
think he's actively herniating."

Dr. Mulligan considered Jason's outlook bleak. She told
Dr. Dunne that she could unscrew the same section of skull
that had been replaced in Baghdad to relieve the pressure on
Jason's brain stem, but that it probably wouldn't help. At the
time, neither doctor knew about Corporal Dunham's emer-
gence from the expectant ward in al Asad eight days earlier.
Later, however, Dr. Mulligan pondered the activity that
Heidi Kraft and the dental team had seen as evidence of re-
sponsiveness, when Jason squeezed their hands and pulled
Heidi to his chest. Dr. Mulligan thought that what had really
been happening was that the injury to Jason's brain was causing him to curl his arms inward. Heidi had been caught up in
a strong, but involuntary, posturing movement that had been
an indication of how bad the damage was, not how much
hope remained. It may even have been that Heidi and the
others had witnessed the moment of terminal herniation,
when the pressure in Jason's brain grew too great to be contained in his skull and pushed downward toward the spinal
column, setting off a brief neurological reaction that was
never again repeated.

"If we don't do anything, he's definitely going to die," Mulligan told Dunne. "If we do do something, there's still a good
chance he'll die." They scheduled surgery for 10:00 a.m. But
they both knew it was not a decision they could make on
their own.

Just before 8 a.m. the phone rang in the Dunhams' room. A
member of the ICU staff told Dan that the doctors wanted to

talk to them about a procedure that Jason might undergo. "If you need to do something to save Jason's life, you do it," Dan said. "I'll sign later."

An hour later Lieutenant Colonel Byrne walked the Dunhams to a windowless waiting room on the third floor. With a little time to spare, they went to Jason's bedside and were troubled to see a group of doctors scatter as they approached. Deb decided to sit on Jason's right this time so she wouldn't have to stare at the more battered side of his face. She thought Jason's neck looked more swollen than it had the night before. Dr. Dunne introduced himself, and Dr. Mulligan joined them back in the waiting room. Deb thought the thirty-five-year-old Mulligan was pretty; Dan thought she seemed awfully young for a neurosurgeon. Dr. Mulligan spent little time on pleasantries.

"The prognosis for your son is grim," she said. She explained that the biggest grenade fragment had caused so much damage that, even if he survived, Jason would likely be paralyzed on one side and unable to speak or understand those who spoke to him. The swelling of his brain stem had destroyed its ability to keep his body alive unless a machine did his breathing for him. "What you see is what you have," she said. "He will never be able to hear you or know that you are there." Mulligan said there was an operation she could do to relieve the pressure in Jason's brain. But, she warned, she wasn't sure that Jason was strong enough to survive the surgery or that it would do any good even if he did survive. The damage, she believed, had already been done and could not be reversed.

"The chances for a full neurological recovery," Dr. Dunne said, "are nonexistent." The doctors then mentioned the unmentionable: the Dunhams should consider taking Jason off life support.

Deb and Dan's fragile week of hope collapsed in an instant.

Dan asked the doctors whether they were certain Jason would never recover. "I can't give you 100 percent, because there are miracles," Dr. Mulligan said. "But I can give you 98 percent."

Dan sensed that the doctors thought he should take Jason off life support. "Are there other patients you can help that are going to make it?" he asked.

"Yes," said Dr. Mulligan.

"Then you'd better do that," Dan said. But it was a leaning, not a final decision. He and Deb asked for time to consider.

"I hate them," Deb said when they were alone. Dan stared at her in shock. "No, not *them*," Deb explained. "Those guys over there that did this to our son." Dan told Deb about the conversation he had with Jason over Christmas, and how Jason had said he didn't want to live attached to a machine. They pulled out a copy of Jason's living will, which he had signed while serving at the sub base in Georgia. They read it together in silence.

If at any time I should have a terminal condition, become in a coma with no reasonable expectation of regaining consciousness, or become in a persistent vegetative state with no reasonable expectation of regaining significant cognitive function, as defined in and established in accordance with the procedures set forth in paragraphs (2), (9), (10) and (13) of Code Section 31-32-2 of the Official Code of Georgia annotated, then, in any such event, I direct that the

application of life-sustaining procedures to my body be
withheld and withdrawn and that I be permitted to die.

"See," Dan said. "This is what he wanted. We have to honor his wishes." At the time, they did not notice a separate Marine Corps document titled "Instructions Upon My Death," in which Corporal Dunham could specify which pallbearers he wanted, what kind of flowers he preferred, and whether he wanted a bugler or color guard. Under "Other Desires or Notes," Jason had written in, "I would like 'Thanks for everything Mom and Dad' put on my headstone."

The Dunhams returned to Jason's room and sat across from each other again, clasping hands. "Give us a sign," Dan begged Jason. "I don't want you to hate me. Give us a sign and help me out."

"He's not going to hate you," Deb assured Dan. "I'm not going to hate you." She looked at the bag of urine hanging from Jason's bed and noticed it was getting darker in color, stained with blood. Jason's right foot seemed to curl inward even more awkwardly than it had before.

Dan needed some air.

When the Dunhams stood up, one of the Marines took their place at Jason's side and held his hand.

<hr/>

The Dunhams wandered the hospital grounds for an hour. Dan looked at Deb, tears streaming down his face. "I know how you feel about Jason. I don't want you to hate me. I don't want anybody to hate me for this. I need to know you're with me."

"I could never hate you," Deb said. "I love you. We have

to help him. He's hurting. He trusts you. I support anything you want to do."

They knew they had made their decision.

They walked to the Fisher House, and Deb crossed the parking lot to the Piners' place. Sarah Piner knew the moment she saw the ashen look on Deb's face that things had gone badly with Jason. They said nothing to each other, but both burst into tears and embraced in the entryway. Sarah sat Deb down in the kitchen. "He's not going to make it," Deb said.

Sarah suddenly felt panicked and at a loss for words. She stepped into the pantry, called Jim at work, and ordered him to come home. "She's here," Sarah said urgently.

When Sarah returned to the kitchen, Deb had snapped into a dazed calm. "Sarah," she asked. "How do I get his uniform?"

"What?"

"His uniform is in California," Deb said. "He's going to want to be buried in it."

Dan drifted alone into the living room, breathing hard. Sarah overheard him talking to himself. "I can't do this," he kept saying. "I can't do this." Jim Piner finally found him on the Fisher House patio. He listened as Dan talked about Jason and about not wanting to take his own son's life. It was an eerily familiar conversation for Jim. He had removed his father from life support after a heart attack. "What would Jason want?" he asked Dan gently.

"That's easy," Dan said. Jason wouldn't want to spend his life hooked up to a machine.

"Well then, I guess that's your answer," Jim said.

Jim drove the Dunhams back to the ICU, where Lieutenant Colonel Byrne was at Jason's bedside, holding his hand. The colonel asked Deb and Dan whether they wanted Jason to immediately receive his Purple Heart, the award given to troops wounded in combat. "I want him to have it now," Deb said. "He deserves it."

Outside the room Dan told Drs. Dunne and Mulligan he had decided to remove Jason's life support. "I need to know what I'm doing is right," Dan pleaded. Jim Dunne said that if Jason were his child, he'd make the same choice.

Lieutenant Colonel Byrne called the office of the Marine Corps commandant, General Michael Hagee, to arrange the Purple Heart ceremony. A lean, blue-eyed man whose blond hair might have been tinged with gray had it been allowed to grow, General Hagee received an e-mail report from the field every time a Marine was wounded or killed, and he frequently visited the injured men at Bethesda to present Purple Hearts. On the afternoon of April 22 Hagee had a meeting of the Joint Chiefs of Staff on his schedule, but he skipped it when he heard that Jason Dunham's parents had decided to remove his ventilator. All he knew about Corporal Dunham from the files was that he had a head wound, so from the back seat of his Cadillac sedan on the way to the hospital Hagee called the Marine commander in Iraq and asked him to collect personal stories about the corporal. The fifty-nine-year-old Hagee had seen men die in combat and comforted the parents of the wounded. Some lashed out at him and the Marine Corps. Some were beside themselves with anguish. Never before, however, had the general sat with parents who knew their son was about to die, and he was nervous about it. But he felt he had to be at the Dunhams' side and wanted to be able to tell them what kind of Marine their son was.

Word of the commandant's urgent request for stories about Corporal Dunham trickled down to Third Battalion headquarters in al Qa'im shortly after 10 p.m. local time. Lieutenant Bull Robinson, Corporal Dunham's platoon commander, was sitting next to his cot when Captain Trent Gibson approached. "Hey, Bull, I need to talk to you," the captain said.

Robinson stood up and reached for his rifle and cap. "Where are we going?"

Gibson looked him in the eye. "Corporal Dunham's not going to make it," he said. Robinson stared at the wall trying to absorb his captain's words. He had heard that Jason was stable enough to travel and assumed that meant he was recovering. Gibson explained that the commandant was going to visit Jason's bedside and wanted to be able to tell Deb and Dan stories about Jason from the Marines who served with him.

Robinson called Fourth Platoon together in the berthing area. Lance Corporal Dean, Jason's close friend since the day Mark returned from leave to find senior Marines living in his barracks room, thought the platoon was getting a new mission. Then he saw tears in the lieutenant's eyes. "I got some real bad news for y'all," Robinson said. "Corporal Dunham's not going to make it. In two hours his parents are going to be taking him off life support."

Captain Gibson assembled the rest of Kilo Company and asked Dean to address the men. "I believe in miracles," Dean said. "Anything can happen in two hours." Dean prayed God would touch Jason and wake him up so he could lead the life he wanted to live. The Marines around him wept openly.

Mark Dean called his wife Becky Jo on a satellite phone and told her that Jason's parents had decided to switch off his life support. They agreed that they would pray simultaneously at the moment they thought the ventilator would be removed. "Things could change," Mark said. "Things could change."

Becky Jo was the only teacher at the day-care center at 1 p.m. in California. A dozen children were napping on mats inside, and Becky Jo went out through the sliding glass doors onto the patio. She paced as she asked God to be allowed to see Jason one more time. "I don't know the situation," she prayed. "I don't know his condition. But I do know You can do miracles. You have a plan for everybody. But why Jason? Why do You want him?"

In the ICU Dan grew shaky and light-headed. The nurses checked his blood sugar, and Lieutenant Colonel Byrne, the head of the Marine liaison office, took him and Deb to the cafeteria. Over lunch the colonel recited a favorite quotation, thought to be from George Orwell: "We sleep safe in our beds because rough men stand ready in the night to visit violence on those who would do us harm."

"Your son is one of those rough men, and you can be very proud of that," Byrne told them. Deb asked him to write the quotation in her notebook.

When the Dunhams returned to the ICU, Jason's right lung had collapsed, apparently from the pressure caused by the ventilator, and the doctors were working to stabilize him. Dan wanted to touch Jason, and he pulled off the surgical gloves. The swelling had spread in Jason's right chest under the skull-and-spade tattoo. Dan thought this was the sign he had hoped for, Jason's way of telling him he had made the right decision.

General Hagee met the Dunhams outside Jason's room. Deb moved to shake his hand; he pulled her into a hug. They spoke quietly for a few minutes. "Your Marine is my Marine, too," the commandant said. "You're part of the Marine family." Then he stepped back and said to his aide, "Let's get this done." The curtain was drawn over the window into the ward, but even those outside the room stood erect when Hagee called, "Attention to orders." His aide read from a certificate:

The United States of America
To All Who Shall See These Presents, Greeting:
This Is To Certify That
The President of the United States of America
Has Awarded The
Purple Heart
Established By General George Washington
At Newburgh, New York, August 7, 1782
To
Corporal Jason L. Dunham, United States Marine Corps
For Wounds Received
In Action
In Iraq on 14 April 2004

Hagee clipped the Purple Heart—a purple ribbon above a gold-edged medal bearing George Washington's profile—on the pillow next to Jason's bandaged head. Then he squeezed Jason's forearm and whispered something in his ear that nobody else heard. He thought about the young man who was about to die.

Dan and Deb stared at Jason from the foot of the bed, too absorbed in their thoughts to hear the ceremony. After it was over, the general embraced Deb, who cried on his creased khaki uniform. Deb stumbled through an apology, and the general reached into his pocket and pulled out a medallion. He explained that many military commanders gave out souvenir coins embossed with their unit or title. He gave his only to those whose performance was out of the ordinary. "I want you to have this," he said. "This is special. This is a Marine coin. This is a part of Jason. I want you to have this to keep with you."

Deb misunderstood. "Do you want me to give this to Jason when we put him to rest?" she asked.

"No, Deb," Dan said. "That's for you." She stuffed it into the pocket of her blue jeans.

Just before the commandant left, Deb told him that Kyle wanted to be a Marine, too, and that she and Dan would support him if that was what he wanted.

———————————

The Dunhams thought Jason's breathing seemed more labored than before, even through the ventilator. "I can't sit here and watch this anymore," Dan told Deb.

Dr. Dunne described how they would disconnect the ventilator, and what would happen afterward. A nurse hooked up a morphine drip to Jason's IV. "Is he going to feel anything?" Deb asked. The doctor assured her that he would not. The Dunhams stepped out of the room. The medical staff pulled the curtain closed, and at 4:35 p.m. the respiratory therapist slid the tube from Jason's throat. The nurse turned off the alarm on his heart monitor.

Deb sat on Jason's right, across from Dan. Dr. Dunne

stood at the foot of the bed watching Jason and the monitors. Lieutenant Colonel Byrne and two of his men stood to the side in silence. The colonel knew he was intruding on a private moment and considered leaving. But this bed was Corporal Dunham's final battlefield, he thought, and Marines don't abandon their brothers on the battlefield.

A chaplain administered last rites. He then leaned over to help Deb remove her gloves, and she once again felt Jason's skin as she held his hand. Sometimes she reached across and held Dan's hand, sometimes she placed her own on Jason's heart. "We're proud of you," Dan said. "We love you."

Deb touched the bridge of Jason's nose, stroked his arm, and said, "It's O.K., honey. You can go now."

Dr. Dunne watched as the blue line on the monitor screen showed plunging levels of oxygen in Jason's blood. His heart rate fell until the green line went silently flat. Dunne stepped forward and bent down to listen to Jason's lungs and heart. He straightened up, removed the stethoscope from his ears, and said, "He's gone." It was 4:43 p.m. on April 22, 2004.

Jason's body relaxed, and Dan thought his son looked like himself again. Deb put a photo of the Dunham family in Jason's hand.

XII | *Home*

Scio, New York

DEB DUNHAM TURNED off the cell phone during their
final night in Bethesda. She and Dan wanted to tell Kyle and
Katie in person about Jason's death, and they didn't want to
have to lie if the children called them before they got home
to Scio. Two Marines in their dress blues met Deb and Dan
at the Rochester airport on the morning of Friday, April 23,
and drove them to Scio Central School. During their short
absence, yellow ribbons, American flags, and red-white-and-
blue banners had sprouted all around the school and along
Main Street.

Kyle was in English class. One of the students glanced out
the window and saw Deb and the Marines walking into the
building. Kyle thought it was good news; if Deb was alone it
probably meant Jason had woken up and Dan had stayed at
the hospital with him. Deb was probably there to pick up
Katie and him and take them to Bethesda. The phone in the
classroom rang, and the teacher told Kyle to collect his things
for the weekend and report to the main office. He ran to his
locker, spun open the combination lock, and grabbed his

backpack. He started to run down the hall, but spotted a teacher and slowed self-consciously to a walk. Outside the school office Kyle saw his mom and dad standing together, and he knew.

"We're sorry, but Jason didn't make it," Deb told him.

Katie left science class assuming her parents' quick return to Scio meant Jason had recovered. Dan saw her coming down the hall and couldn't fathom how to tell an eleven-year-old that her big brother, her idol, had died. He put his arms around her and said, "His injuries were too bad, and he had to go to heaven." The Marines stood guard outside the principal's office while the Dunhams held each other inside, then Dan walked Katie back to class to drop off her three-ring science binder and get her backpack out of her locker. The Dunhams bundled into the back seat of the Marines' SUV and drove by the minimart, through the stoplight, past The Store and the Mahogany Ridge, over the Genesee River, and home. After they left, school administrators announced Jason's death over the public address system and asked that everyone give the Dunhams the weekend alone.

Four hours' drive away, in Vandergrift, Pennsylvania, Justin Dunham was out knocking on doors, trying to sell vacuum cleaners. He and a couple of colleagues stopped for an early lunch at a Chinese restaurant, and he stepped outside when Dan called his cell phone. "Are you at work?" Dan asked. "Is your boss there?"

"No," Justin said.

"Is somebody else there with you?"

"Yes."

"Let me talk to him." Justin went back inside and handed the phone to a colleague, but he had already guessed that Dan had bad news to tell him and just didn't want him to be alone when he heard it. When Justin got the phone back, Dan said, "We want to tell you something. Just relax. Your brother passed away last night."

Natalie, Jason's biological mother, hadn't seen or talked to him since his graduation from high school in 2000, and she hadn't known he was in Iraq. When Deb returned from Bethesda, she left a message for Natalie's mother, who got in touch with Natalie's husband Jim. Jim went to the Seneca Falls bank where Natalie worked. It was a Friday, and there were lots of customers at the teller windows. "What do you want?" Natalie asked. "I'm busy." Jim told the news to one of Natalie's coworkers, who walked around the counter, took Natalie's key, locked her cash drawer, escorted the couple to an office, and closed the door.

"Something has happened," Jim said.

"What?"

"Jason." Natalie broke down in tears. One of the bank vice presidents called his pastor, who came to the bank, but Natalie couldn't focus on what he was saying. She was bitter that nobody—not Deb, not her own mother—had told her Jason had been wounded.

Dan and Deb didn't know Natalie's phone number, but Natalie called Deb in a fury that night. "Tell me what happened."

"Jason's dead," Deb said. Dan listened from across the room, angry that after so many years Natalie suddenly seemed to care about Jason.

But as the week went on, Dan softened a bit. He and Deb

were surrounded by those who adored Jason; Natalie had so few Jason memories to share. She stayed at a motel in Wellsville the weekend of the memorial service. During visitation hours at the funeral home on Friday, April 30, Natalie felt the hostile stares of many of those who passed by Jason's casket, and stayed only briefly. She watched as Dan, Deb, Kyle, Katie, and Justin shook hands with strangers and hugged friends in the reception line. "She's grieving for what she never had," Dan told Deb. "You're grieving for what you lost."

Afterward Deb took Justin aside. "Thank you for choosing me to be your mother," she said.

"There was no choice," Justin replied. "You were always our mom."

Saturday, May 1, 2004, dawned gray and rainy. The pallbearers—Jason's brothers Justin and Kyle, his buddy Jud Lambert, and others—rolled the casket down the hallway at Scio Central School and into the gymnasium. They came to a stop under a basketball hoop that had been raised to the ceiling for the memorial service. Folding chairs filled the center of the gym, covering the snarling Scio tigers in the jump-ball circle. The bleachers had been rolled out. Deb, Dan, and their families sat in the front. Sara Walters, Jason's girlfriend, was grateful that Dan and Deb wanted her to join them; she felt it was the nicest thing anyone had ever done for her. Members of the Scio Central School class of 2000 sat in reserved seats behind the family. All but a few of the thirty-seven graduates showed up, and they had spent most nights that week at the Mahogany Ridge toasting Jason with beer and shots of cinnamon schnapps.

In a village of 1,900 people, 1,500 were stuffed into the gym that day.

The reverend told the crowd that he hadn't known Jason well and had asked Deb for a few Jason stories to help him prepare. He held up the seven single-spaced typed pages of memories she had given him, stories of stolen cookie dough, high school pranks, and family devotion. Jason had never hung up the phone or left the house, she wrote, without saying, "I love you."

The sun came out at Fairlawn Cemetery, and the residents of Scio stretched a giant American flag along Main Street. Dan put a wad of chewing tobacco in his mouth for the slow walk up the hill. Seven Marine riflemen stood near the gravesite. They fired three salvos, and a bugler played taps. The Marines folded the flag that had been on Jason's coffin into a crisp triangle and handed it to Dan. The Marines saved three empty shells, one to be tucked into each corner of the folded flag.

In early September, Natalie drove back to Scio, stopped at the Kmart to pick up a few things, and met Deb at Jason's gravesite at the top of a soft slope. As she always did, Deb wore Jason's dog tags on a chain around her neck and carried the commandant's coin in her pocket. There were two polished black granite stones at the gravesite. One had Jason's name etched into it, alongside the Marine Corps logo and motto, Semper Fidelis—Always Faithful. On the other stone were engraved two hearts joined by wedding rings, and Deb's and Dan's names, their deaths foretold by the dashes that followed their birth years. They didn't want Jason there alone. Deb gave Natalie a set of Jason's desert fatigues and a Purple Heart pin, a gold star on a purple background surrounded by a wreath. They hugged, and Natalie said, "Thank you for taking such good care of him."

"That was the easy part," Deb replied. "Thank you for having him."

"You," Natalie said, "were his real mother."

The Dunhams received hundreds of letters from people they knew and people they did not. In June they received one from Elia Fontecchio, the Kilo Company gunnery sergeant who had cradled Jason's fragile head in the medevac Humvee as it raced to Landing Zone Parrot. "I prayed [the] injuries he sustained would not take his life. Even though I knew he couldn't hear me, I gave him words of encouragement," Elia wrote from al Qa'im.

> I'd like to share a dream I had with you. It took place about a week after his passing. I had just awaked and I saw myself sleeping among the men in Fourth Platoon. I look across a row of men and saw Jason sleeping next to one of his friends. He awoke shortly after me, as did everyone else, and began telling his story of recovery. It was very good to see him so well and happy again . . . He is very missed.

Six weeks after writing the letter Elia Fontecchio was killed when a buried artillery shell exploded next to him as he waited for his Marines to climb aboard his Humvee near the Euphrates River.

"My heart goes out to you during this most difficult time in your lives," Roberta Sherman wrote the Dunhams.

Of the lives saved that day, one was my son, William Hampton. He has only spoken about Jason once to me. Jason was an example to many of those men especially of the new "boots" who went over with them and his team. He will always remain in our hearts and prayers.

It is so difficult to be grateful and yet so very sad for the loss you all feel.

I pray that your pain will be lifted.

Deb wrote back and told Roberta about her own experience a month before Jason was wounded. She and Dan had woken up to the news that Third Battalion had taken casualties. She wept all morning until she called the base at Twentynine Palms and was told that if she hadn't received a call or visit yet, then Corporal Dunham was just fine. She was swept first by relief, then by shame. "I felt such a wave of guilt at that moment because I was grateful that my son was alive and that other families were not as lucky as I was," Deb wrote to Roberta. "We have prayed that William and Kelly would recover.

"When you next get a chance to hug your son please give him one from me. He does not need to know it is from me, but I would appreciate if you would do that for me."

Lance Corporal Bill Hampton's nightmares began in the hospital in Baghdad. In the dreams, he'd be back on that dirt lane in the H-K Triangle, the Iraqi would lunge for Corporal Dunham's throat, Bill would lean down to jab the Iraqi with his rifle barrel, the grenade would explode. Bill would wake up gasping. Then he'd fall asleep and dream it all over again. Later, waiting in California for the battalion to return from Iraq, he took on a part-time job helping his girlfriend cater a Fourth of July party. Bill sold smoothies, cotton candy, and snow cones. But the fireworks reminded him of AK-47 fire, artillery, and mortars, and he found himself frightened and incapacitated by the booms. He sat on a cooler while his girlfriend held him and told him everything would be all right.

Bill wanted to talk to Dan and Deb, but couldn't bring himself to call, unsure what he would say to them if they answered the phone. When they finally met at the battalion's annual Marine Corps Birthday Ball after the troops returned home, Bill couldn't look Dan in the eye. Bill didn't know why; he just knew that he wasn't ready to let go of his pain. "You did all you could," Dan assured him. "This is just the way it was meant to be."

Deb became long-distance friends with Linda, Pfc. Kelly Miller's mother. "We believe that Kelly and William are both very special," Deb wrote Linda. "I do not know what is in their futures but I (we) firmly believe that Jason did what he had to do and they have some important purpose here and he has his to do in Heaven."

Kelly underwent two emergency surgeries after he got home to Eureka and continued to suffer from nerve damage to his left arm. He was short-tempered with his girlfriend Shannon and had the same recurring nightmares as Bill Hampton. Kelly rarely spoke of the incident in the H-K Triangle, yet it weighed ceaselessly on him that Jason had given up the rest of his own life so Kelly could finish his. Kelly felt he should have been the one to die. After all, he was the point man and just a private first class, a boot. Dunham was a corporal. At the end of July, Kelly downed a couple of beers and stopped Linda in the hallway of their house. "Mom, goddammit, I should have done more to save Jason," he said. "I should have."

Lance Corporal Falah spent months undergoing treatment at the San Diego Naval hospital. At night he dreamt that he jumped into the swimming pool at his father's apartment building only to realize that the pool was filled with blood and the faces of the dead were crowding around him—his parents, his friends, and Lieutenant Colonel Lopez. He woke up sweating, shivering, and screaming. Between nightmares and fits of rage, he worried that his arm wouldn't recover sufficiently to allow him to stay in the Marine Corps.

By mid-May, wounded Iraqi prisoners were beginning to stack up at the Eighty-first Detention Facility tent at the U.S. air base in Balad, and Colonel Allen Alleman, a doctor from the Washington State Army National Guard, took it upon himself to try to figure out which of his charges should be sent to more secure prisons and which were civilians who should be released. One of those on his list was Enemy Prisoner of War #549, the man shot by the Marines as he drove past the Crackhouse in Husaybah. In an e-mail, the colonel asked the Second Medical Brigade for permission to release a civilian with a gunshot wound to the neck; an elderly, nearly blind and deaf civilian with shrapnel wounds to the chest; and EPW #549, Ahmed Jazzim Zein, "a civilian, arrived April 22, with abdominal and back wounds."

"He is fully recovered and ready for release," the colonel wrote, adding that there was nothing in the files to indicate he was an insurgent. The Second Medical Brigade sought the advice of Task Force 626, a secret unit made up of special operations troops and CIA operatives to hunt down top-level insurgents. The task force had no evidence that Zein was anything other than a civilian and authorized the colonel to let him go.

Zein had been belligerent and suspicious when he arrived at the detention tent, but he had gradually grown friendlier, especially toward Specialist Jerry Orona, a National Guard medic who had been working in construction in Tacoma when he was called up. Through an interpreter, Zein told Specialist Orona he missed his family and had been studying to get into the oil industry. On May 31, six weeks after he was shot, Ahmed Zein shook hands with each of his fellow inmates. Jerry Orona took him to the air base gate and gave him a handful of sunflower seeds, a bottle of water, two one-dollar bills, and a Meal, Ready-to-Eat. Ahmed kissed Jerry on both cheeks, an Arab tradition, and an interpreter drove him away to catch a ride back to Husaybah or wherever home might have been.

Kilo Company Marines sealed the tattered remains of Corporal Dunham's helmet into two large plastic bags and placed them in a metal storage locker in the company command post in al Qa'im. Captain Gibson soon caught wind of Corporal Dunham's theory about grenades and helmets, and he pieced together what had happened on April 14. He went straight to Lieutenant Colonel Lopez. "Hey, sir, I think Dunham may have put his helmet on that grenade," Gibson said.

"If that's true," Lopez replied, "then he should be written up for the Medal of Honor." He ordered Captain Gibson to investigate.

Staff Sergeant Ferguson had no doubts whatsoever about what had happened that day. But he thought that it might be hard to get Dunham a medal without eyewitnesses. He hoped that Lance Corporal Hampton's and Pfc. Miller's wounds would turn out to be light enough that they'd soon return to the battalion to tell the story. But after a few days it was apparent that the wounded men wouldn't be back. Ferguson sat down with Lieutenant Robinson and Captain Gibson in the Kilo Company command post, where Corporal Dunham had spent the night writing his first and only patrol order. "I think we should shoot for the Medal of Honor," the staff sergeant said.

The Medal of Honor, created during the Civil War, is the nation's highest award for military valor, saved for those whose actions are considered so self-sacrificing, so risky, so far beyond the requirements of duty that nobody would have criticized them for choosing to do something else instead. Just 3,459 such medals had been awarded, 296 of them to Marines, and it is the only medal that requires the president's personal approval. Until the Iraq war, the most recent act deemed worthy of the honor had occurred in 1993, when two Delta Force snipers died trying to protect a downed Blackhawk helicopter crew in Somalia. Few in the military have ever witnessed an act that warranted the Medal of Honor, or even met someone who had a Medal of Honor. But the medal's mystique pervades the military. Each barrier on the obstacle course at the Marine recruiting depot at Parris Island, South Carolina, where Jason Dunham sweated through boot camp, is named for a past Medal of Honor recipient. As the recruits run the course, the drill instructors lecture them about how getting past each obstacle requires the virtues of the medal recipient for whom it was named. But everyone knows the classic way to earn the Medal of Honor is to jump on a grenade to save your buddies.

Lieutenant Robinson and Staff Sergeant Ferguson drafted the award citation on behalf of Fourth Platoon, describing what had happened that day in the H-K Triangle. Captain Gibson put together a report on Mills Bomb hand grenades. At Twentynine Palms, Lieutenant Huerta interviewed Pfc. Miller and Lance Corporal Hampton. And Lieutenant Colonel Lopez signed a letter to the regimental commander recommending Corporal Dunham for the award.

> *Corporal Dunham's courage and sacrifice was far beyond the call of duty. In the confusion of battle he was unhesitant in his leadership and advance toward the enemy. Realizing the enemy possessed a hand grenade Corporal Dunham may have been able to avoid his fatal wounds by simply moving away. However, this was not the way this non-commissioned officer led. There was an enemy to engage and his Marines were in danger. I deeply believe that given the facts and evidence presented he clearly understood the situation and attempted to block the blast of the grenade from his squad members.*
>
> *His personal action was far beyond the call of duty and saved the lives of his fellow Marines. He is worthy of the highest recognition and honor of our nation.*

The nomination quickly secured the support of the top Marine commanders in Iraq, who sent it on to their superiors for review, a process expected to take many months or even years.

Third Battalion said good-bye to Corporal Dunham on April 28. The Marines gathered in the parking lot outside the command post at al Qa'im, a former office building of the Iraqi railroad company. Staff Sergeant Ferguson called roll for Fourth Platoon, each Marine responding to his name by saying, "Present." When the staff sergeant called, "Corporal Dunham," there was silence. Lance Corporal Castaneda, one of Dunham's point men, stepped forward and plunged a rifle bayonet first into a sandbag. Staff Sergeant Ferguson called the name again, "Corporal Jason L. Dunham," and Polston, the boot, placed a pair of desert-tan boots in front of the rifle. "Corporal Jason L. Dunham," Ferguson called a final time. Lance Corporal Gummi Bear Covarrubias placed a Kevlar helmet on the rifle butt. Taps played over the loudspeaker.

Lance Corporal Mark Dean told the assembled troops a story about the trip that he, Becky Jo, and Corporal Dunham took to Las Vegas shortly before they shipped out for the war. Sitting in the hotel room, Corporal Dunham told the Deans he was considering extending his enlistment so that he could stay in Iraq through the battalion's entire tour, instead of going home early.

"You're crazy for extending," Lance Corporal Dean said. "Why?"

"I want to make sure everyone makes it home alive," Jason said.

SOURCES AND ACKNOWLEDGMENTS

The Gift of Valor is based mostly on interviews with the men and women who played a role in Jason Dunham's story. With very few exceptions, such as the wounded Iraqi civilian and Ayad the injured translator, I interviewed every person named in the book, as well as many who do not appear in the text. I began researching Jason's story while in al Qa'im a few weeks after his death and continued through the rest of 2004. Memories are, of course, flawed, especially in the confusion of battle. Even official records are often inaccurate or contradictory. I have made every attempt to corroborate each person's recollections with those of others present at the same place at the same time. When quotations are used to describe conversations, I have tried to verify them with all participants. All descriptions of people's thoughts and states of mind come from the people involved, of course, and when possible I have reviewed those descriptions with them more than once to ensure accuracy. Many descriptions of place, personality, Marine culture, and other details come from my observations and reporting during four periods I spent in Iraq with Third Battalion, Seventh Marines, in 2003 and 2004, as well as during visits to al Asad, Baghdad, Balad, Landstuhl Re-

gional Medical Center, Ramstein Air Base, the National
Naval Medical Center in Bethesda, Twentynine Palms, Scio,
Eureka, and Las Vegas.

I also relied on letters, essays, personal journals, and medical records, as well as documents related to Jason's Medal
of Honor nomination. Additional information on the medal
came from the Congressional Medal of Honor Society, and
some of the history of al Asad air base came from www.global
security.org. *The Village*, by Bing West, provided fascinating
background on the Marines' experiments with combined action platoons in Vietnam. *Making the Corps*, by Thomas E.
Ricks, piqued my interest in covering the Marines and
helped me understand their unique society. Some information on the Israeli experience treating head wounds came
from B. Brandvold, L. Levi, M. Feinsod, and E. D. George,
"Penetrating Craniocerebral Injuries in the Israeli Involve-
ment in the Lebanese Conflict, 1982–1985: Analysis of a Less
Aggressive Surgical Approach," *Journal of Neurosurgery* (January 1990). 1st Sgt. Daniel Hendrex of the Third Armored
Cavalry Regiment was very helpful in describing the Army's
experiences and practices in Husaybah, Karabilah, and al
Qa'im.

To fill out the history of Scio, New York, I tapped the
vast knowledge of Cheryl Smith, Frank O'Brien, Phyllis
Young, and Mary Havens, as well as the 1961 unpublished
manuscript "The History of Scio" by G. Coats, D. Farwell,
D. Lambert, and D. Lewis. For the other Scio, I consulted the
speeches of Daniel Webster.

I borrowed from my own articles in *The Wall Street Journal* for details and, on occasion, phrasing when describing
Marine snipers, hand-to-hand combat training, and a few

other aspects of Jason's story and the Marine experience in Iraq.

I owe an incalculable debt of gratitude to Deb, Dan, Justin, Kyle, and Katie Dunham and their extended families for their candor, generosity, and patience during the many months I worked on this book and asked them to relive the most painful experience a person could imagine. To have Jason's story put to paper cannot relieve their grief, but I hope at least I have filled in some blanks for them and done justice to his life and to theirs.

It should also be evident that without my access to Lt. Col. Matt Lopez, Capt. Trent Gibson, and the men of Third Battalion, Seventh Marines, this book would never have seen print. I am deeply grateful for their willingness to allow me to ride with them to war and for their good humor, openness, and, frankly, protection while I did so.

The Marines, sailors, soldiers, airmen, and civilians named in this book made it possible to tell Jason's story. Many others not mentioned spent hours with me as well, sharing their experiences or simply making sure I got on the right helicopter or Humvee going to the right place. I mention some of them here and apologize if anyone has slipped through the cracks.

In the Marine Corps: Lt. Gen. James Mattis, Col. Craig Tucker, Col. Jenny Holbert, Lt. Col. Michael Belcher, Lt. Col. T. V. Johnson, Maj. Anthony Henderson, Maj. George Schreffler, Maj. Jason Johnston, Maj. James Kendall, Maj. Tim Keefe, Maj. Ray Hamlin, Capt. Dominique Neal, Capt. David Romley, Capt. Mike Hudson, 1st Lt. Rudy Salcido, 1st Lt. Eric Knapp, 1st Lt. Wayne Mai, 1st Lt. Victoria Jennings, Sgt. Maj. Daniel Huff, 1st Sgt. Michael Templeton, Gunnery Sgt. Adam Walker, S. Sgt. Houston White, S. Sgt. (ret.) Angela Cronan, S. Sgt. (ret.) Willie York, Cpl. Mike Padisak, and Cpl. Armando Rodriguez, who stuck with Jason until the very end.

In the Navy and at the National Naval Medical Center: Capt. Kermit Booher, Lt. Cdr. Chito Peppler, Lt. Ted Hering, Master Chief Ronald Kunz, RP2 Monica Kuhl, Becky Kunz, Corey Schultz, and Albert Harrison.

In the Army and at Landstuhl Regional Medical Center: Maj. Robert Knetsche, Maj. Eric P. Carnahan, Maj. James B. Milburn, Maj. Cathy Martin, Maj. Richard Spiegel, Capt. Cathy Wilkinson, the dogged Capt. Jeff Greenlinger, Capt. Laura Ricardo, Capt. Randall Baucom, 1st Lt. Shawn Tulp, 2d Lt. J. Thomas Larson, CW2 Billy Grindstaff, CW2 Roderick Petersen, CW3 John Wuensche, and the imperturbable Marie Shaw.

In the Air Force and Air National Guard: Lt. Col. Fred Nelson, Maj. Eric Weissend, Maj. Stanley Martin, the resourceful Capt. Shellie Russell, and T. Sgt. Brian Jones.

Drs. Jeffrey Poffenbarger, Richard Gullick, James Dunne, and Lisa Mulligan were kind enough to answer endless and often repetitive questions about the brain and Jason's condition and treatment.

In Scio, I benefited greatly from conversations with Mike Pavlock, Kyle Young, Tim Smith, and Judy Consedine.

My editors and colleagues at *The Wall Street Journal* enabled me to spend long months reporting from Iraq and made sure the stories I sent back were coherent, accurate, and, most importantly, published. For that I am very thankful and want to mention with appreciation Paul Steiger, Jerry

Seib, David Wessel, Phil Kuntz, Helene Cooper, Greg Jaffe, Mike Miller, and Carrie Dolan.

Yochi Dreazen, Sara Schaefer-Munoz, June Kronholz, and especially Nicholas Kulish were kind enough to read over my drafts and had no trouble finding ways to improve them. Any errors, however, remain my own.

My agent Marly Rusoff is the greatest ally an author could want. My editor Charlie Conrad at Broadway Books had the vision, when I did not, to see that Jason Dunham's story could become a book and the persistence to track me down in the desert to make it happen.

Felix, Ann, Diana, and Arthur Phillips have always been there for me, and I have always needed them.

I dedicate this book to Julia, Tashi, and Alice Maud. How did I get so lucky?

ABOUT THE AUTHOR

MICHAEL M. PHILLIPS, a staff reporter for *The Wall Street Journal*, has done four tours in Iraq with the Third Battalion, Seventh Marines. He lives in Washington, D.C., with his wife and two children.

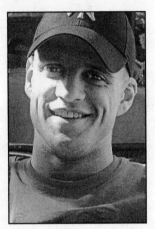

Jason L. Dunham
1981–2004